Empty Promises

This book is dedicated to my
colleagues in the Equality
Authority who worked
with such dedication and
creativity to make it
what it was

Empty Promises

Bringing the
Equality Authority
to heel

Niall Crowley

A. & A. Farmar

British Library Cataloguing in Publication Data
A CIP catalogue record for this book is available from
the British Library

ISBN: 978-1-906353-21-6

First published in 2010
by
A. & A. Farmar Ltd
78 Ranelagh Village, Dublin 6, Ireland
Tel +353-1-496 3625 Fax +353-1-497 0107
Email afarmar@iol.ie

Cover photograph by Melanie Reidy
Printed and bound by GraphyCems
Typeset and designed by A. & A. Farmar

Contents

Acknowledgements

Thanks—

To Bride Rosney for her early encouragement and support.

To Sabrina Mc Nern, 'Mary', Phyllis Fahey, Mervyn and Richard, Joan Salmon and Edward Reilly for their courage and for their generosity in sharing their insights and perspectives on taking a discrimination case.

To Siobhan Bigley, Pat Normanly, Sheera Mehlman, Jack Keyes, Bride Rosney and Dorinda Ryder for their commitment and for their generosity in sharing their insights and experiences in building more equal organisations.

To Melanie, Liam and Lorcan for taking the leap into the unknown with me.

To Anna Farmar for her early enthusiasm and interest and her expert editing support.

To Atlantic Philapthropies and the Joseph Rowntree Charitable Trust for enabling me to complete this book.

Preface

'DO YOU WANT TO DRIVE THE EQUALITY AGENDA?' was the title on the job advertisement It was February 1999—and I did. The Public Appointments Service was seeking a chief executive officer for the soon to be established Equality Authority. So off I went to buy a suit. I spent the Easter holiday reading up every report on equality issues I could lay my hands on.

I was ready for the interview. It was a disaster, in my opinion. The interview panel seemed to want a manager for the new organisation whereas I presented as a driver for equality. I put the suit away and swore I would never wear it again. But I did wear it again—at the opening of the Equality Authority in October 1999. I got the job.

Three linked experiences had brought me to this point. The first was my involvement as a part-time volunteer for four years from 1977 with the Simon Community. This was at a time when the organisation was deeply influenced by its founder Anton Wallach Clifford. His philosophy was one of accepting homeless people as they were and being with them in their daily struggles, as opposed to attempting to change them. The Simon Community offered me a way out of the segregation from the realities of inequality and poverty that comes with a comfortable middle-class background. It allowed me to engage with homeless people as part of a community and to share in a limited way their struggles, humanity and exclusion. It was a politicising experience.

My day job at the time was as a civil engineer. It provided little opportunity to give practical expression to what I was learning from being involved in the Simon Community.

This influenced my decision in 1982 to join a state construction company in Mozambique for four years—the second experience. Mozambique only gained independence from Portugal in 1975. Its government was socialist. It sought to break with the damaging dependence of most developing countries on the wealthy and industrialised world, and worked to develop an economy at the service of a more equal society. My time in Mozambique allowed me to imagine alternative ways of economic, social and cultural development—alternatives with a capacity for achieving a more equal society.

The third experience was the period of twelve years I spent with Pavee Point Travellers Centre on my return to Ireland. Pavee Point advanced a new understanding of Travellers as a minority ethnic group. We worked to combat the racism experienced by Travellers and to promote a new model of integration with the settled community, a model based on making adjustments for cultural diversity, rather than on demanding that the Traveller community assimilate. Organisations in the public and private sector were challenged to take account of the practical implications of cultural diversity in the way they went about their business. My experience in Pavee Point showed me that institutions had to change if the inequality, racism, and poverty experienced by the Traveller community were to be overcome.

My appointment at the Equality Authority was a surprise to many. *The Irish Times* (4 June 1999) pointed out that I lacked any legal or civil service experience. *The Sunday Business Post* (6 June 1999) carried a headline on my appointment: 'equality chief swapped cigars for social justice'. A comfortable middle-class background was not supposed to lend itself to a concern for equality.

Some colleagues in the community sector were a bit taken aback at my transfer to the statutory sector with which I had often clashed on Traveller issues. The civil service was probably equally surprised. A staff member of the Equality Authority reacted with some amusement in an early conversation, saying to me 'They never thought they'd get someone in this job who actually believed in equality'. I got the impression he felt I was not going to last very long.

In the event , I was chief executive of the Authority for ten years, from its foundation until I resigned in November 2008 in protest at a 43 per cent reduction in our budget.

This book charts the neutering of the Equality Authority, a statutory body which was at the height of its ambition and performance when its ability to carry out its mandate was compromised. It is a story of media backlash, opposition from vested interests, and the waning of political support for the equality agenda. It is also the story of some of those who took cases under the equality legislation and of others who made use of the legislation to develop effective equality and diversity systems in their organisations. These are the people who gave life to the equality legislation. Through their courage and determination they ensured that it contributed to a more equal Ireland. These are the people who are left isolated and without necessary support with the diminution of the Equality Authority.

Finally, the book looks to the future and seeks to define the parameters of the policy change that is now required to move away from the current neo-liberal model towards a more equal Ireland.

1. The equality infrastructure

The equality movement

Ireland was late to address the broader equality agenda, but when it did, initially at least, it did so in an ambitious and innovative way. So much so that, briefly, it was a leader in the field. At the turn of the century, as we entered the 2000s, Ireland had become a European leader, rather than a reluctant follower, in the drive for a more equal society. It had taken pressure from the European Union (EU) before we introduced legislation to establish an entitlement to equal pay between women and men (1974) and to prohibit discrimination by employers on the grounds of gender and marital status (1977). But with the establishment of the Equality Authority and the Equality Tribunal under the Employment Equality Act 1998, and the expansion of their functions under the Equal Status Act 2000, Ireland moved to the forefront on these issues within the EU for the first time.

The legislation that finally established the Equality Authority in 1999 followed years of lobbying on the part of various groups. In 1990 the Irish Council for Civil Liberties made a case for anti-discrimination legislation 'to encode an open-ended prohibition against discrimination on the basis of sexual orientation'. At the same time, various Traveller groups were becoming more assertive in seeking anti-discrimination legislation. In *Anti-racist Law and the Travellers*, published in 1993, the Irish Traveller Movement and others pressed the case for legislation that 'would go beyond punishment of individual acts of discrimination. It must also deal with the structural nature of discrimination.'

Women's groups, gay and lesbian organisations and disability organisations were also pressing the need for similar legislation. A broad community sector coalition formed to combat a wide range of injustices by lobbying for the enactment of anti-discrimination legislation.

The participants in the social partnership process were also committed to advancing the equality agenda. This process, which had started in 1987, had always been about more than pay and conditions of employment. National agreements had also contained significant social policy aspirations and commitments. By the 1990s four pillars within the partnership process had been defined: the business, trade union, farming, and community and voluntary sectors. The newest pillar, the community and voluntary sector, included organisations articulating the interests of groups experiencing inequality such as women, older people, Travellers and people with disabilities. In 1993 the National Economic and Social Forum (NESF) was established, as part of the social partnership process, specifically to explore policy initiatives in respect of employment, equality and social inclusion. The Forum produced a ground-breaking report in 1996, *Equality Proofing Issues*, (Forum Report No. 10, February 1996) which included specific recommendations on the content of employment equality and equal status legislation.

In 1993 the coalition of Fianna Fáil and Labour produced a Programme for Government that responded to this growing constituency. It ambitiously committed the government to 'eliminating inequality for all groups in society that have suffered from disability, disadvantage or discrimination'. Eventually this led to the publication of the Employment Equality Bill 1996 and the Equal Status Bill 1997. Although these Bills were passed by the Oireachtas, certain clauses, including those requiring employers and service providers to make reasonable accommodations for people with disabilities, were regarded as suspect under the Constitution, and were referred by President Mary Robinson to the Supreme Court. The Court found that these clauses were unconstitutional, so new legislation had to be drawn up.

As it happened, the government had changed in the meantime and now consisted of the Fine Gael, Labour and Democratic Left parties. Redrafting of the two Bills took some time, and it was not until a further change of government, this time putting Fianna Fáil and the Progressive Democrats in power, that the legislation was finally passed in revised form. These turns of the political roundabout meant that all of the political parties in the Dáil, with the exception of the Green Party and Sinn Féin, had been directly concerned with sponsoring this legislation. It was not, therefore, a party-political issue.

Thus Ireland became a European leader on equality issues in response to a broad-ranging demand for a more equal society.

Grounds of discrimination in equality legislation

Earlier equality legislation had made discrimination on the grounds of gender and marital status illegal. The new equality legislation of 1998 added seven further grounds: family status, age, disability, sexual orientation, race, religion and membership of the Traveller community. One glaring omission was socio-economic status. There is significant class-based inequality and discrimination in Ireland in a wide range of areas, including the labour market, education and access to medical services. Despite this omission, the more comprehensive response in the new equality legislation to inequality and discrimination did seek to cover an impressively broad range of groups at risk of discrimination.

The legislation also required the government to review the grounds covered within two years to make sure that the legislation was indeed comprehensive, and such a review was initiated in 2001. At this time, the Equality Authority, Congress and the community and voluntary sector recommended the inclusion of four further grounds: political opinion, criminal conviction, trade union membership, and socio-economic status. However, as we shall see, times were changing and ambitions waning. Michael McDowell, who was Minister for Justice, Equality and Law Reform at this time, did not appear to have any appetite for broadening the equality agenda.

Scope of equality legislation

The new equality legislation was designed to be holistic in scope as well as comprehensive in the grounds it covered. The Employment Equality Acts prohibit discrimination in the workplace and in vocational training. The Equal Status Acts prohibit discrimination in the provision of goods and services, accommodation and education. They also include provisions on registered clubs. The legislation covers organisations in their relationships with both employees and customers. Previous equality legislation had been confined to the workplace and vocational training. With time it became clear, however, that there were shortcomings to the scope of the legislation.

In 2001 a Traveller took a case under the Equal Status Acts against the Garda Síochána. Four horses had been found wandering on a public road in Gort and the Traveller was prosecuted because he owned one of the horses. He alleged discrimination, claiming that the other horse owners were not prosecuted because they were settled people. The Equality Tribunal, established to decide cases under the legislation, found that the equality legislation did not cover the investigation and prosecution of a crime by the Gardaí (DEC-S2001-011). It covered services provided by the Gardaí but, unlike in Britain and Northern Ireland, it did not cover their controlling functions. The Equality Authority recommended that the scope of the equality legislation be expanded to include the functions of the state, particularly in the areas of policing and immigration. However, the appetite for expanding the scope of the legislation had also clearly waned by then and no progress was achieved.

Nonetheless, the enactment of the Employment Equality and the Equal Status Acts did mark a dramatic, if imperfect, new departure in the promotion of equality and the combatting of discrimination. The legislation offered new forms of redress to members of a wide range of groups experiencing inequality and discrimination. It served as an effective lever for those advocating equality within their workplaces and organisations. Above all, it reflected the political establishment's apparently committed affirmation of equality as a core societal value, its acknowledgement of the diversity in the make-up of Irish society and its demand that discrimination not be tolerated.

Belfast Agreement

John O'Donoghue, Minister for Justice, Equality and Law Reform, placed the legislation in the context of the 1998 Belfast Agreement, when he spoke at its enactment. He noted that both the Employment Equality Act and the Equal Status Act responded to specific commitments made by the Irish government in the Agreement. He claimed that 'Equality of opportunity in all social and economic activity is a right safeguarded in the Good Friday Agreement'. The Agreement requires the Irish government to ensure 'at least an equivalent level of protection of human rights as will pertain in Northern Ireland'. But the legislation enacted in Ireland actually afforded a lesser degree of equality protection than prevailed in Northern Ireland.

In particular, legislation in Northern Ireland includes

a requirement on the public sector to have due regard to equality in carrying out its functions. Designated public sector bodies are required to produce equality schemes (plans for promoting equality of opportunity) in their roles as employers, service providers and purchasers of goods and services. There is no such requirement in the Republic, though the obligation to draw up equality plans might have succeeded in reducing the number of allegations of discrimination made against the public sector. No action has been taken to ensure equivalence of protection north and south in this area of equality.

Equality Tribunal

The Equality Tribunal was established under the Employment Equality Act of 1998, as a distinct quasi-judicial body. It is the first forum for those seeking redress under the equality legislation. It hears, investigates and decides claims by those alleging discrimination. The Tribunal also offers mediation of claims.

The Tribunal's investigative function is important. It means that people can present or defend a case without needing to have the ability to marshal evidence or make complex legal arguments. Unlike in a traditional court setting, the equality officer of the Tribunal plays a proactive role in establishing the facts and the relevant legal arguments. It is also useful that the Tribunal does not make any orders for costs in cases before it. All this enhances its accessibility.

Although established with quite different mandates, the Equality Authority and the Equality Tribunal are often confused with each other, or seen as the one organisation. This confusion is not helped by the fact that they share a building in Clonmel Street in Dublin. It was surprising to find that even legal firms made this mistake, sending the Authority letters that should have been addressed to the

Tribunal. Some media commentators exploited this confusion in an attempt to diminish the organisations. Kevin Myers, for example, wrote inaccurately about the 'Imams of the Equality Authority, who by an extraordinary dereliction of duty, were allowed by the government of the day to appoint their own inspectorate, their own prosecution service, and run their own courts' (*The Irish Times* 4 June 2003).

Equality Authority functions and main activities

The legislation gives the Equality Authority three functions:

1) to combat discrimination and promote equality of opportunity in the areas covered by the equality legislation: the workplace, vocational training, the provision of goods and services, accommodation, education and registered clubs;

2) to provide information to the general public on the provisions of the equality legislation; and

3) to keep the equality legislation itself under review and to make recommendations to the Minister for Justice, Equality and Law Reform for any changes that might be necessary.

In the Authority we identified four strands of activity in implementing this mandate: enforcement, development, research and communication. Each strand had its own separate section within the Authority.

Enforcement work principally involved providing legal advice and assistance to people who feel they have been discriminated against under the equality legislation. This was the biggest section, with sixteen staff in 2007, which was the high point in the Authority's life to date.

Development work focused on initiatives that assist employers and service providers to take steps to promote equality, to make adjustments for diversity and to eliminate discrimination in their organisations. Ten staff worked in this section in 2007.

Research work included exploring the situation of groups experiencing inequality and discrimination, and establishing a case for investing in equality and diversity systems and initiatives. Four staff worked in this area in 2007.

Communication work involved disseminating information on the equality legislation to the general public, and promoting equality as a core societal value. This section had thirteen staff in 2007.

In addition there was the administration section, with thirteen staff in 2007, oiling the wheels.

The staff at the Equality Authority belong to the civil service. Although we recruited a small number of staff from the non-governmental sector and the legal sector, most of the staff were seconded directly from the Department of Justice, Equality and Law Reform. Some came from other government departments, others were transferred from the old Employment Equality Agency, our predecessor body, and some were newly recruited civil servants on their first assignment. This is not best practice. International standards set by bodies such as the Council of Europe's European Commission against Racism and Intolerance require that specialised equality bodies, such as the Equality Authority, be free to recruit their own staff. This power can be important for the effectiveness of the body, and for its ability to secure necessary specialist skills. In practice the Equality Authority was both independent and effective. The staff became deeply committed to the clients and to the organisations that the Authority worked with. They became expert and innovative in the work, and loyal to the institution we were building and developing.

It took time, however, for a united team to emerge. With people coming from different backgrounds, inevitably there were battles concerning the nature, style, and ethos of the Authority. Typically these contests were cultural in nature and, although important, were fought over seemingly trivial issues such as the operation of the canteen, the computer system or the way individuals in different grades related.

The Equality Authority developed through these contests as a place where people were happy to work, where they were able to take on responsibilities that matched their skills rather than being confined by grades, and where people related well to each other. Each staff group brought its own specific experience, traditions, and values to the melting-pot. The positive nature of the culture that emerged was most evident when staff who had been transferred out of the Authority met up with old colleagues. It could be heard in wistful reminiscences of what they missed from their time working there. The product of this culture was an ethos and value system in the Equality Authority that stimulated and engaged staff, that enabled them to be productive and creative and that allowed them to build an organisation that was both independent and effective.

2007: the high point

The year 2007 marked the high point in the Equality Authority's work. Our public information centre responded to 3,047 queries on the Employment Equality Acts and 1,559 queries on the Equal Status Acts. This was a rise of 2.6 per cent on the previous year in the number of people seeking such assistance from the Equality Authority. We opened 80 new cases under the Employment Equality Acts, 107 new cases under the Equal Status Acts and 17 new cases under the Intoxicating Liquor Act. Overall, in 2007 we held 737 case files under the three Acts (Equality Authority *Annual Report* 2007).

This work, however, reflected only the tip of the iceberg

of discrimination. In 2005 the Central Statistics Office (CSO) published a special survey which reported that 12.5 per cent of the population aged eighteen or over, amounting to over 380,000 people, said that they had experienced discrimination in the previous two years. The CSO also found that 60 per cent of those who said they had experienced discrimination did nothing about it and only 6 per cent took any formal action in response to it (Central Statistics Office, 2005a. *Quarterly National Household Survey, Equality Module*). These figures showed both the relevance of the Acts and the scale of the challenge if the objectives of the legislation are to be achieved.

During 2007 the Authority published research with the National Centre for Partnership and Performance which explored the business case for equality. For the first time in an Irish context, the impact on business of investing in equality and diversity systems was quantified. The research showed that workplace equality and diversity systems improved labour productivity, workforce innovation and employee retention (*New Models of High Performance Work Systems, The business case for Strategic HRM, Partnership and Diversity and Equality Systems*, National Centre for Partnership and Performance and Equality Authority).

During 2007 we ran five national public awareness campaigns to publicise the equality legislation, to promote a culture that espoused equality as a core value and to highlight the Authority's work. The campaigns promoted work-life balance, the value of diversity, anti-racism in the workplace, adjustments in service provision to enable access for people with disabilities and saying no to ageism. That year also, the Authority published new work on the issue of gender stereotyping in the advertising of toys for children. From this we developed an initiative to challenge other forms of stereotyping. at work, in public sector service provision and in advertising and the media.

Practical support was given to 103 small and medium enterprises to develop their equality and diversity systems. With EU funding we also established an equality main-streaming unit to support organisations providing voca-tional training to promote equality, make adjustments for diversity and eliminate discrimination in their work. A new initiative was developed with the Irish Business and Employers Confederation (IBEC) and Congress to assist employers and trade unions in creating integrated work-places where migrant workers were employed.

Internationally, 2007 was the European Year of Equal Opportunities for All. The Authority was given a high pro-file at the first EU High Level Equality Summit held in Berlin and it was cited as an example of best practice in a research study published in 2007 by the European Commission on the issue of multiple discrimination.

Approaches to equality

All these activities give a flavour of the organisation that had been built over the years since its establishment in October 1999. These were exciting times with new promise for advancing equality in Ireland, and a sense that, while the work was only beginning, progress was being made. However, the new consensus on the importance of equal-ity and diversity and on the need to tackle discrimination, marked by the legislation, did not mean that the concept of equality itself ceased to be contested. The consensus did not go so far as to establish what level of equality we as a society sought to achieve. This has been the focus for ongo-ing contest since the Equality Authority opened its doors.

The dominant approach to equality is that of promot-ing *equality of opportunity*, with the emphasis on the indi-vidual, fairness and tolerance. Minimum entitlements are to be afforded to all individuals and competition for ad-vantage after that is to be governed by fairness and non-discrimination. It is an approach that acknowledges the diversity of individuals and promotes a tolerance of this diversity.

The problem with this approach is that it accepts and co-exists with significant and persistent inequalities. It seeks to regulate or manage inequality rather than to eliminate it. Although competition for advantage is regulated by fairness, already existing disadvantage is not eliminated. Thus this approach can serve to justify inequalities. It is supposed that fairness prevails and everyone is able to make his or her own choices, and further it is presumed that little more can be done to improve the situation of those who experience inequality. The fault is therefore incorrectly deemed to lie with those experiencing inequality. Tolerance as a response to diversity also raises questions. Tolerance is about putting up with something that is problematic. It does not require any understanding of diversity and can easily co-exist with contempt for difference.

An alternative approach to equality seeks to secure *equality of outcome* and to develop a *valuing of diversity*. This approach focuses on the disparities and inequalities between groups in society. It sets out to achieve substantive and real change in the experience and situation of groups experiencing inequality. This is not about enforcing sameness on individuals or groups, rather it is about offering them meaningful choices between real options.

If we are to achieve a more equal society we need to change the systems and structures that currently shape society, the way society organises itself and the way organisations go about their business. This change must include a new response to diversity, in which difference is valued as a source of benefit and creativity. Organisations need to take account of the practical implications of difference. This approach to equality was endorsed in *Equality Proofing Issues*, the 1996 National Economic and Social Forum report in which the social partners recommended 'that equality objectives should focus on seeking to achieve equality of access, participation and outcome in relation to employment and non-employment areas'.

Equality Authority approach

The Equality Authority's mandate is to promote equality of opportunity and to combat discrimination in the areas covered by the equality legislation. However, although the equality legislation largely follows an equality of opportunity approach it is not confined to this approach. For example, it contains provisions that allow for positive action to achieve full equality in practice in the workplace. These provisions, which reflect an equality of outcome approach, enabled us to keep to our mandate while pursuing an ambition to achieve real change and improvements for groups experiencing inequality. A focus on equality of outcome was most evident in our developmental work supporting good practice in the workplace and in the provision of goods and services. We enjoyed valuable support and encouragement in this work. A wide range of organisations from all sectors worked with us in these initiatives to progress equality.

To give a sense of what equality and equality legislation mean for individuals, and the difference that courageous people can make in the drive for a more equal society, the next chapter tells the stories of people who had the strength to take cases against those who had discriminated against them and shows the importance of the support they received from the Equality Authority. Chapter 3 looks at the vital role played by a number of champions of equality within their organisations and how the equality legislation and the Equality Authority served as a lever for change.

2. Tales of courage

Those who criticise the equality legislation often refer to what they see as unbridled litigiousness. Kevin Myers, for example, suggested, in the *Irish Independent*, that the Equality Authority has 'done more to provoke the compensation culture than any other Government funded body' (17 July 2007).

In fact, few people take any formal action to challenge discrimination they experience. Most people do nothing at all. 'Head down, keep going and don't make yourself vulnerable' is the order of the day; 'nobody in Ireland thanks a trouble maker' is the accepted wisdom. As we have seen, fewer than one in seventeen of the people who say they have been discriminated against make a formal complaint or take legal action (Central Statistics Office, 2005a, *Quarterly National Household Survey*, Equality Module).

It takes some courage to bring forward a case under the equality legislation. There is a personal investment in taking the legal route—almost as if you are putting yourself forward for judgment. Taking a case is counter cultural in Ireland where dissent is seen as a problem. There is the risk of being treated badly or disadvantaged in some way by the organisation you take the case against. There is therefore something special about those who use the legislation to challenge the discrimination they experience. There is also something important about the contribution they make. There is personal gain for them in that by winning their case they can be vindicated, their experience of discrimination can be addressed and financial compensation for the effects of this discrimination can be secured; but there is also a wider impact that goes beyond the individual taking the case. People who take cases demonstrate that change is possible by making use of the equality legislation. They show that injustice and discrimination do not have to be tolerated. They provide leadership for others who experience similar discrimination. They promote the standards that have to be observed by all employers and service providers under the equality legislation.

The following tales of courage introduce some of the people who have taken cases under the equality legislation. They explore their motivations in taking a case, the barriers they faced, what kept them going and the impact the whole process had on them. They help us to better know and understand that one person in seventeen who takes it on himself or herself to respond formally to the experience of discrimination. They should help identify what needs to be done for more people to be able to effectively challenge the discrimination they face.

Sabrina McNern

In 2001 Sabrina McNern was sacked from her job in Blooms Hotel because she was pregnant. She was no activist. She described herself at the time as gullible and trusting in people. The discrimination threw her life into crisis. She felt there must be someone who could help. However, it was only a somewhat random call to directory enquiries that brought her to the Equality Authority.

It was anger that sustained her through the process of taking a case. She had a lot of doubts. A few times she thought of pulling the plug on the case and she was fearful of offending anyone. But then she would think back to the way she was sacked. Her boss had taken her to a nearby pub. He told her that the business was in trouble and that he had to let her go. She remembers an almost moral tone to the conversation, as he kept referring to her pregnancy as her 'predicament', which did little for her self-esteem.

She was asked to tell no one and she felt almost as if she had done something wrong. However, her boss had given her new opportunities when she got the job in the first place. She was grateful for this and she felt sorry for him thinking he was going to have to close his business. It was a shock then to find the hotel advertising jobs in the paper shortly afterwards. Sorrow was replaced with anger at having been betrayed.

She went on to try for other jobs. One employer, impressed with her CV, rang her to offer her a job. She told him she was expecting a baby. He just said he was sorry but he couldn't take her on. She was stuck in the house all the time then and began to despair. She went to the county council to see if she could get some form of social housing. All she got was a telephone number for the homeless section which she was to ring when she had the baby. She went back to her family in Donegal to have the baby and split up with her partner for a time.

Anger alone wasn't enough to bring Sabrina through the process. It was her partner who pushed her to take action, saying that what was happening to her wasn't right and there must be someone who could help. She decided to take a claim for discriminatory dismissal on the gender ground under the Employment Equality Acts against Blooms Hotel to the Labour Court. The Labour Court was the institution that dealt with such claims at the time. Her parents never commented on the case. The legal route wasn't their way of doing things. But her father came with her to Dublin every time she went to deal with the case. The Equality Authority provided her with legal advice and representation—not just legal support from her solicitor but moral support and encouragement to keep going.

Sabrina was successful in her case. The Labour Court found that Blooms Hotel had discriminated against her because she was pregnant. She was awarded €15,000 in compensation for the discrimination—close to the maximum award possible. The scale of the award and the publicity the case generated served as a deterrent to this type of discrimination by other employers. This was valuable because pregnancy-related discrimination is widespread. It is one of the biggest issues in the casework of the Equality Authority under the gender ground of the Employment Equality Acts. In Britain, research by the Equal Opportunities Commission in 2005 found that almost half of all pregnant women experience some form of disadvantage at work and estimated that some 30,000 pregnant women are forced out of their jobs each year.

It wasn't about the money for Sabrina. She does say she would have loved to have seen her boss write the cheque, just to get it through to him what he had done. But she calls it 'dirt money', and after one trip to the shops to buy clothes she never wore, she spent the money on others around her. The case was about fighting for other people who might find themselves in the same situation and were less lucky in being able to take it on. She drew strength from seeing herself as fighting for others and this kept her going through the case. 'It wasn't just about me'. There was a lot of media coverage after the case which she found difficult. However, she had always promised herself that if she won she would stand up and speak for those who were less lucky.

Sabrina has extraordinarily detailed recollection of the discrimination she experienced. Eight years after it happened each conversation and development in the case was related as if it only happened yesterday. She says she is a stronger person for taking on the case and fighting for what was right. She feels 'if I can do that I can do anything'. The hearing in the Labour Court gave her the chance to tell her story and to see her employer's representatives embarrassed as they were forced to try and justify what they had done.

'Mary'

Unlike Sabrina, Mary (not her real name) is an activist. Before taking a case to secure adequate provision for her disabled son, she had been employed in an Irish centre in London. She was an active trade unionist in London, serving as shop steward; she marched in support of the miners' strike in Britain.

Mary was a tenant of the local authority. In 2001 she applied under the Disabled Person's Alteration Scheme for an extension to her house to provide additional space that was needed by her son on foot of his having autism. Her application was refused. The local authority appeared to treat her application as an overcrowding issue and rejected it. She could not believe what was happening. Her first reaction was that it was her fault. She thought she must be making a mistake in her application. When it hits you in your personal life, she says, 'you are paralysed'.

All the advice Mary got was to 'leave it, this is the way things are—you won't get anywhere if you take it on'. Gratitude is what is expected from those getting services for people with disabilities, not demands. She says it only 'came up on her gradually' but she took on the challenge.

Mary appealed the refusal twice. She remembers being told by one of the officials that she would get no grant from him as long as there was a pensioner in the area still needing a hand rail. This, she says, was so blatant that it 'got her fire going'. She won her appeal but her application was only accorded a low priority level.

She persisted and got the local authority to send an architect out to her house. The architect told her that the house seemed fine for an extension and that this is what would be recommended in the report. Then she was told by the local authority that the architect's department had said the extension was not feasible. This lie, she says, was a further source of her strength through the legal process. She feels that the local authority's understanding of disability was limited to physical disability and that the officials feared they would 'open the floodgates' by responding to the needs of a person with autism.

With the support of the Equality Authority Mary took a case to the Equality Tribunal on the disability ground under the Equal Status Acts. She had heard of the Authority through the media and had thought it 'a fantastic and progressive development' (with some foresight, she had also thought 'give them enough rope and they will end up hanging themselves') but she was still surprised when a statutory body took on the case. She felt she was able to do 75 per cent of what was needed to take a case but she could not do the legal bit. She found the legal advice and representation provided by the Equality Authority to be vital.

Mary won her case. She was awarded €6,350 which is the highest award possible under the Equal Status Acts. The equality officer of the Equality Tribunal who heard the case expressed considerable concern at how the local authority had misrepresented the architect's report. Most importantly the local authority was ordered to either build the extension to Mary's house or to provide alternative accommodation suitable to her son's needs within a year.

Mary takes huge pride in the house she finally secured from the local authority and in particular at the way it caters for her son's needs. But although she had won her case and the matter was supposed to be resolved within a year of the Tribunal's decision she had had to keep fighting. Nothing had changed in the local authority. In fact she felt they just got nastier. She says that 'winning the case just brought the fight to the next level. It took another two years until I secured this house. The local authority only eventually responded under the threat of more legal action.'

The local authority first offered her a bungalow in her estate. It was what she calls 'a poisoned chalice'. It was in the worst part of an estate where her son had already been terrorised. She refused it, and it is telling that this house still stands vacant. She felt she was back in the grip of a bureaucracy that was set on managing her and on deciding for her what she wanted and needed. 'It was like playing poker with them, except they knew all the cards and would only show some of them.' She fought on until a suitable house was finally offered.

The case brought back Mary's old trade union negotiating days to her. 'I had lost my fight since then.' She could fight with ease for others but 'when it comes to your own family and children it is too raw. There is no distance and it is all emotion. The stakes are really high.' She found her day in court 'brilliant and amazing'. It was important to see those who had blocked her 'from getting justice' for over six years, those who told her she would never get this house, having to 'answer for their lies and the barriers they put in my way'. She appreciated the chance to be heard, to say how it was, to recount her experience. She didn't think she was going to win but felt 'the fight does not end here if I lose the case, it is for life'.

The fight does go on too. Her son will leave school when he is eighteen. She says there 'is nothing for him as once they are eighteen they go into adult services, services that don't understand autism and that are no more than a glorified child-minding service'. She is now in battle with the HSE—another organisation 'holding all the cards and only showing those that suit them'.

Phyllis Fahey

Phyllis Fahey says she 'only got brave when her husband went into hospital'. Like Mary, she is engaged in an ongoing battle with the HSE. Her husband is in long-term care, and a number of problems have arisen, concerning drug prescriptions, unexplained fractures, weight loss and neglect, which Phyllis is determinedly pursuing. Before that she was not good at dealing with confrontation. She remembers back to a time she worked in a bank branch in Britain. She uncovered a fraud. The bank did not appreciate her action and tried to transfer her out of the bank. It was her first experience of bullying. She couldn't deal with it and had to leave. She is a stronger person now, though, and says that 'when you get to seventy you don't give a damn. I've got to the stage when I won't take rubbish.'

Her battles with the HSE have given her an awareness of how older people are perceived in society and the negative stereotypes held about them, reinforced by the media. She makes particular reference to the portrayal of older people in advertisements and to news coverage where file shots of older people's legs shuffling around in care settings are used as illustration for news stories. These issues fuelled her response to the discrimination she experienced at the hands of Ulster Bank.

In 2005 Phyllis decided to change her car. She went to a car dealer and put down a deposit on the car. She then called Ulster Bank in Maynooth, where she had had a deposit account for ten years, to get a loan. She was told that the bank did not give loans to people over 65 years of age. Later the manager rang her to apologise and to say that they had no discretion in this policy as they had to obey the rules of the Financial Regulator. Phyllis didn't want to go around to the car dealer to cancel the purchase in case he would think she 'was on some sort of blacklist' but she had no choice. She was 'embarrassed, hurt and belittled' by Ulster Bank's treatment of her.

Then she got to thinking about the anti-ageism law she had heard about on the Pat Kenny show. She rang Ford Credit and her credit union to see what their policies were.

Neither of these organisations had an upper age limit on providing loans. She felt she 'had been made an idiot of by Ulster Bank with their talk of banking rules'. She got a loan from her credit union and bought a car.

Age and Opportunity, a non-governmental organisation of older people, guided Phyllis on what to do and where to go. She took a case to the Equality Tribunal on the age ground under the Equal Status Acts against Ulster Bank with the support of the Equality Authority. At first she agreed to try the mediation service offered by the Equality Tribunal. However, she felt patronised by Ulster Bank in this process and they failed to respond in any real way to her concerns. She decided to go ahead with the case.

Phyllis emphasises the importance of the legal support provided by the Equality Authority when she describes seeing Ulster Bank's legal team lined up against her — 'they must have cost a fortune'. Her son came with her to the hearing. At one point he advised her not to lose her temper as the bank's legal team tried to undermine her story. She says she just 'told the story as I told it three years ago. I was composed, told the truth and knew that the truth will out.'

Ulster Bank was found to have discriminated against Phyllis and was ordered to pay €2,000 in compensation. The legal process took three and a half years, which did put pressure on Phyllis. However, it was worth it. 'The result was great. The coverage was really positive. People rang me who I hadn't seen in years.' She says it 'gave people courage' and tells the story of a friend who told her she was thinking of Phyllis when she complained about a problem she was having due to ageism. There was a photo shoot outside her home for the newspapers. Local children gathered wanting to know what it was all about. They wondered if it was some sort of drugs bust. Phyllis told them to watch out for the news because it was about 'Grannies rule OK'.

The case was a matter of principle for Phyllis. 'People

talk down to older people,' she says. 'It is very patronising.' Older people can be made powerless in the face of powerful organisations like the banks and the HSE. This has to be challenged and Phyllis used the media coverage of the case to encourage older people to challenge discrimination when they face it: 'Don't be afraid. Take them on.'

Phyllis went on to play a valuable role in the campaign to challenge the proposed merger of the Equality Authority and the subsequent cutback to its funding. She used her experience of taking a case to good effect in highlighting the need for an independent and effective Equality Authority.

Mervyn and Richard

Principle was also at the heart of the case taken by Mervyn, who is from Northern Ireland, supported by his partner Richard, who is from the Republic. They have been together for twenty years. Their relationship has been recognised in Northern Ireland under the Civil Partnership Act 2004. This, says Richard, has emboldened them in their identification as a couple. However, Richard feels that the 'denial of us as a couple' in Ireland has a 'strong emotional resonance'. All of this made the case they took deeply personal.

Mervyn has a terminal illness. He was on invalidity pension when in 2005 he applied to the Department of Social and Family Affairs for an adult dependent allowance. This allowance is payable to unmarried heterosexual couples under the invalidity pension. Mervyn had been given two years to live and Richard had left work to care for him. The application was refused. Mervyn and Richard were very upset at this refusal. Richard describes it as 'a huge kick in the teeth'. It also had practical implications. Richard had to return to work, Mervyn's care was interrupted, and both men suffered significant stress.

Richard had been involved in gay rights issues as a

student. Mervyn had been involved in Christian pro-gay activism. Both men have 'a sense of civil liberties' and are 'used to standing up when something is unjust' even though they find this personally demanding. However, taking this case was still not an easy decision as 'it is harder when it is about yourself'. Taking a case also raised the question of coming out, as neither man is out to all members of his family. There was also the added factor of Mervyn's illness and how the stress of a case might affect him.

They thought long and hard before jointly deciding to take a case to the Equality Tribunal on the sexual orientation ground under the Equal Status Acts with the support of the Equality Authority. Their expectations had been raised by the recognition of their relationship under the Northern Ireland legislation, according to Richard. The deciding factor, according to Mervyn, was that 'there had to be others in similar circumstances and, thinking of the wider gay community, someone had to make the effort'.

Richard was buoyed by a sense of optimism as he had heard many cases were successful. In hindsight he felt this was 'undue optimism' as he learned that the case would be won on points of law rather than the injustice of what had been done. Mervyn was 'appalled to discover that in relation to social welfare schemes the Government thought it had given itself a total exemption from its own equality legislation'. This was in reference to a very broad exemption in the Equal Status Acts for actions taken on foot of other legislation—an exemption that in effect allows the Government to legislate to discriminate.

Mervyn and Richard had heard of the Equality Authority through the newspapers. They had experience of working in the welfare systems of Northern Ireland and Ireland and both are college educated. However, the legal complexity of the case could be 'mind blowing' for them at times. The prospect of a court hearing was 'intimidating'. They feel the support of the Equality Authority made the case possible and helped them to proceed with it. They found the staff 'professional, sympathetic and pleasant'.

The case was settled before it went for a hearing to the Equality Tribunal. In October 2006 a Government decision was made to make a payment to the couple (which included arrears due because of the initial refusal of the allowance), and to process their application for the adult dependent allowance provided the standard criteria were met. The Minister for Social and Family Affairs said this was not to be a precedent.

The success of the case gave them a great boost. Richard describes how he 'felt vindicated' and that they 'had struck a blow for gay equality'. The successful outcome of their case was important to Mervyn in that the Minister for Social and Family Affairs 'recognised us as a couple'. Richard emphasises the success of the case in 'precipitating state acknowledgement of the entity called a "gay couple"'. Mervyn felt the recognition of them as a couple was a precedent and, in a media statement, called on the Minister to fast track any other applications of a similar nature. He also said the Government should bring in civil marriage for gay and lesbian couples without delay.

They are both still disappointed with the slow progress in introducing civil partnership legislation in Ireland. They recognise that 'civil marriage is the only thing that offers absolute equality'. They are also concerned that the proposed legislation in Ireland falls short of that in Northern Ireland, in particular in that lesser provision is made for children of same-sex couples. Civil partnership has a very immediate importance for them as Mervyn states his 'determination to hang in until Richard knows he can be eligible for widow's contributory pension'.

Taking the case re-awakened their interest in rights issues and enabled both Mervyn and Richard to rediscover their energy to engage in lesbian, gay, bisexual and transexual (LGBT) issues. They have been involved in a range of events on these issues, have worked to support a recognition of lesbian, gay and bisexual people in the Christian Church, and have joined the Equality and Rights Alliance which is campaigning to challenge the budget cuts made to the Equality Authority.

While encouraged by the success of their case Mervyn and Richard are both conscious of the risk that they took. They would have felt very differently if they had lost the case. Richard says that 'if unsuccessful I would have felt so demoralised and rejected. There is a huge personal investment in a case like this. This is a risk that is not widely understood.' The case was very personal and Mervyn describes how 'emotionally involved with it I was' and emphasises the 'emotional risk' involved in taking the case.

Joan Salmon

Joan Salmon is, like Mervyn and Richard, very conscious of the risks involved in taking a case. Joan, who is blind, is a successful para-equestrian rider and won a bronze medal in the 1996 Atlanta Para Olympics. In July 2001 she was selected by Para Equestrian Ireland to attend a training event in Scotland but was told she could not bring her guide dog with her because of Government restrictions due to an outbreak of foot and mouth disease. Joan checked this and was informed by both the Irish and the Scottish Departments of Agriculture that there would be no problem bringing her guide dog. Para Equestrian Ireland then said that bringing her dog would create too much work for the person accompanying the team. Joan made alternative travel arrangements but was then told her place had been given to another rider.

Joan considered this to be discrimination. She had not heard of the Equality Authority, so she raised the matter in the media and called on the person she was dealing with in Para Equestrian Ireland to consider her position. Para Equestrian Ireland barred her from entry to all future events under their control until she made an unreserved apology to the person concerned. She did write a letter of apology in September 2001 but she was told it was not an unreserved apology.

There was a core principle at play here for Joan—the principle of independence. She says that 'when I lost my sight, learning to be independent, being independent, feeling independent and being seen to be independent became all important. Before my blindness it was a matter of personal choice.' She notes that 'dependence on others brings varied emotions—there is the feeling of genuine gratitude and then the feeling of the duty to feel and demonstrate gratitude.' Para Equestrian Ireland 'think they are doing good and this made it difficult to take on the organisation. Because disabled people are dependent on them they think we should do things the way they say.' She points out more generally that 'helpers can disempower those they help by the abuse of power and control.'

She tells the story of a previous incident with Para Equestrian Ireland that raises the same issues of power, control and independence as the incident in 2001. Joan uses a system of callers to guide her around the dressage arena. It is a system that has attracted much interest from teams in other countries. At an event in Denmark Para Equestrian Ireland decided to use the system of a single caller. Joan was told she could not bring her team of callers. She would not have been able to compete without them. Her team had to come of their own accord and still found they were excluded from what the rest of the Para Equestrian Ireland team did in Denmark.

In recounting the experience of not being allowed to bring her guide dog to Scotland, Joan says she 'was left with the choice of either accepting passively what was being done for fear of further reprisals and further withdrawal of voluntary services, or of making my complaint official and in the public domain where hopefully the response had to be honest, just and fair.' When the reprisals came it was her friend Deirdre Bangham who pointed her towards the Equality Authority and supported her in taking a case of victimisation to the Equality Tribunal under the Equal Status Acts.

Most of the riders 'go with the flow' and don't raise issues or make complaints. Deirdre describes Joan as a 'gutsy person, someone who is strong, determined and focused'. These personal attributes were important in helping her to take on Para Equestrian Ireland. Deirdre points out that Joan 'knows when she is being patronised'. Joan herself emphasises 'that you have to see the fight has a chance of getting somewhere, before you take it on'. She is very focused on her riding and has the high standards of all top athletes. 'I know what I want, I have standards and won't be walked on . . . there are times when the issues at stake are too important for any conflict to be swept under the carpet by grinning and bearing the status quo.'

It was difficult for Joan to take on Para Equestrian Ireland. It is the gatekeeper for riders to qualify for international para equestrian events. The organisers held the power and she knew she would lose out. They are 'well meaning and well intentioned'. But all too often good intent requires gratitude and is averse to challenge. A revealing point is made in this regard in the decision of the equality officer of the Equality Tribunal, who found against Joan, when he stated that 'Having considered the evidence before me at great length and having listened to accounts of the assistance and support which was given to Ms Salmon in the past by the PEI and its voluntary members, I find myself concurring with the PEI's view that [the person mentioned in the media reports] deserved an unreserved apology from Ms Salmon for the personal comments made about her in print.' Good works being done on a voluntary basis clearly came into play in the consideration of the case.

Joan appealed the decision to the Circuit Court with the assistance of the Equality Authority. The case was heard in May 2004. She found the experience 'nerve wracking' and found it very difficult being up in the witness stand. However, she was 'delighted and over the moon' when the Circuit Court found that she had been victimised by Para Equestrian Ireland. The Circuit Court ordered Para Equestrian Ireland to pay her €3,500 in compensation, to readmit her to membership and to allow her to participate in their events.

Joan points out that this victory not only 'got me back in but also set a standard for other people to see—a standard that says don't sit back and be walked on.' She sees the outcome as a boost for independence for people with disabilities and as an encouragement for a new approach to working with people with disabilities by voluntary organisations.

She explains the need for new approaches because 'unless help and support is given within a climate of unconditional positive regard, with mutual respect and with the acceptance of the individual's right to question and challenge, then there is the potential for gross abuse of power and disempowerment of the individual.' Deirdre says there is a problem with the disability sector in this regard where 'people are well intentioned but can't see people with disabilities as equals' such that they end up controlling rather than enabling people.

Both Joan and Deirdre maintain that the issue is still not closed. Joan says 'it was hard going back after winning the case'. She still does not feel included in Para Equestrian Ireland. She has been back riding and people have been

'pleasant . . . [but] they feel hard done by . . . the only reason I am back is because they were ordered to have me'.

Edward Reilly

When his job ended in April 2003, Edward Reilly went to
his local health centre in Tallaght to apply for payment of
supplementary welfare allowance. His claim was processed
normally and a cheque was sent to him by post. In May he
went back twice to the local health centre, once to query
the amount he had been paid and again to query the non-
receipt of a cheque. He was then told that they didn't deal
with Travellers in his local health centre and that he would
have to go to a central unit in Castle Street in Dublin city
centre to process his claim. He remembers that 'when they
thought I was a settled person I got very understanding
treatment. But then the attitude changed when they knew
I was a Traveller'.

He knew it was discrimination and he asked the Irish
Traveller Movement to ring up the local health centre but
this did not change anything and from then on he had to go
to Castle Street to get his allowance. His wife Winnie Reilly
remembers Castle Street as 'a most degrading place. They
don't look at you as a human being. They weren't listening.
They just looked at you as "another Traveller"'. The service
was 'much slower going to Castle Street' than that provided by the local health centre.

Traveller organisations had been arguing for the closure
of Castle Street ever since it was established in 1984. It was
a segregated and centralised system to provide supplementary welfare payments to all Travellers in the greater
Dublin area. They had argued that it was a poor service, in
unsuitable buildings and discriminatory in its segregation
of Travellers.

Edward and Winnie both have a strong sense of justice. They have been engaged in ongoing struggles with

their local authority to secure suitable accommodation that meets their needs as Travellers and the needs of their children, one of whom has an intellectual disability. They know that 'you can get a reputation and you can be punished for that'. They are careful in how they take issues on. Still they won't simply accept injustice or discrimination.

Edward knew about the Equal Status Acts from a course he had taken in Clondalkin and he wanted to take the matter further. The Irish Traveller Movement put him in contact with the Equality Authority and he took a case on the Traveller community ground to the Equality Tribunal against the HSE with the support of the Authority. It 'was nerve wracking' to take a case, he says, because 'we weren't sure where we fitted into social welfare' once the case had started.

The case went on for over four years. Edward remembers more than a few times 'getting onto the Irish Traveller Movement to get onto the Equality Authority' to find out what was going on. Over this time Edward and Winnie had to continue using the services in Castle Street. They found the staff more polite 'which was unbelievable in Castle Street' and felt that they 'knew they could lose this case . . . they were trying to make sure Travellers would still want Castle Street'.

It was very much a team effort for Edward and Winnie. Edward says 'I opened the barrier . . . She provided the backbone.' However, the hearing in the Equality Tribunal was 'frightening'. They got some confidence when they went into the hearing room and 'saw the faces of the people from Castle Street'. Edward says that 'They had no legal team. That's how insignificant they thought we were. We could see them whispering and their expression changed when they saw how organised we were.' Winnie says 'the case was going on for years. Why were they not better prepared? They didn't put up a good defence.' The equality officer of the Equality Tribunal who heard the case was also not impressed. One of her conclusions was that 'the respondent's position that the service evolved to cater specifically for the needs of the Traveller community is simply not borne out by the evidence presented'.

The Equality Tribunal's decision was published in July 2007. The HSE was found to have discriminated against Edward. It had to pay the maximum compensation to Edward and was ordered to make his supplementary welfare allowance payments to him at his local health clinic. The HSE was also ordered to arrange payment of supplementary welfare allowance to Travellers at all outlets at which such payments were available to settled people.

Edward and Winnie take an obvious pride in what they have achieved. Edward says he was 'delighted' and that the 'case broke Castle Street'. Winnie says 'We weren't after the money. We were told there would be no compensation. It was more the principle of winning the case.' Edward confirms this: 'We took it for the principle.'

Edward is still concerned that the issue is not fully closed. There can be a danger for Travellers of being segregated within service provision to the general public with Travellers being automatically allocated to the one official, as well as by separate provision of services to Travellers. He thinks the Traveller site where he lives is 'under the one person' in the local health centre. Winnie agrees and says her 'belief at the moment is that this site is being segregated'. She adds that 'if only one person is on Traveller sites that's discrimination'.

These tales of courage come from a diverse group of people. Sabrina McNern says she 'did not have a clue about the equality legislation'. Mary was an experienced activist with a history of involvement in rights issues. Phyllis Fahey had grown from being 'hopeless in dealing with confrontation'.

Both Mervyn and Richard came to their case with a 'developed sense of civil liberties'. Joan Salmon refuses to be 'walked on and can't understand why people would do this'. Edward Reilly was driven by a strong sense of justice. Despite this diversity a coherent and shared spectrum of motivations emerges from these stories that ranges from the personal to the societal.

Some of the cases were motivated by the need to solve specific personal problems created by discrimination. Mary secured the accommodation she needed to cater for her son's particular needs. Joan got back into Para Equestrian Ireland so that she could continue to compete in the events it controlled. Edward and Winnie no longer had to travel to Castle Street which Winnie described as 'a degrading place'.

Personal vindication also emerges as a strong motivation. Phyllis felt she had 'been made an idiot of' by the Ulster Bank manager and his talk of banking rules. Sabrina was 'angry at being betrayed' when Blooms Hotel advertised for posts after she was sacked. The need for leadership in a context of injustice also emerges as a motivation. Mervyn and Richard knew there were couples in a similar situation to theirs and felt 'someone had to make the effort'. Joan wanted to set a standard for other people to challenge injustice—'don't sit back and be walked on'.

Wider societal goals underpin the motivations in all these cases. Mervyn and Richard felt they had 'struck a blow for gay equality' and secured a crucial 'state acknowledgement for that entity called a "gay couple"'. Sabrina took strength from a sense that she was 'standing up for other people who might be less lucky' than her. Edward was delighted to win because his case 'broke Castle Street'. Phyllis wanted to challenge the way 'people talk down to older people and patronise them'. Joan sought to assert an independence for people with disabilities, particularly in their dealings with voluntary organisations, so that they can get help and support in a context of 'mutual respect and with the acceptance of the individual's right to question and challenge'. Mary was also concerned with power relations and sought to challenge the way public sector bureaucracies engage with the people to whom they provide services.

These stories depict a context that is not very supportive of people seeking to exercise their rights. There is little evidence of any culture of rights. Mary was told to 'button up, you need these people'. Joan felt the 'other riders just went with the flow'. Sabrina describes people in the rural area she was from as 'just taking discrimination and going on about their business, because most people know people as friends'. The unsupportive culture evident in these stories needs to be challenged. A culture where it is seen as normal to question, challenge and complain in the face of injustice is needed to support the effective implementation of equality legislation.

The wider field of policy making can influence the emergence of a more supportive culture. Mervyn and Richard point out how the introduction of the UK Civil Partnership Act emboldened them in taking their case and raised their expectations. Legislation, Government policy and public sector programmes that communicate a valuing of and respect for diversity and equality build confidence among members of groups experiencing inequality that it is safe and valid to assert their identity and to challenge any injustice visited on them due to their identity.

It is not easy to take a case under the equality legislation. One immediate and striking difficulty is the time taken to conclude the cases. It took Mary eight years from her initial compliant until she got her new and suitable house. She points out that 'justice delayed is justice denied'. Phyllis identified the length of time as a pressure. She says she rang the Department of Justice, Equality and Law Reform at one point to say the 'case has taken three and a half years already, I'm seventy-four and I might be dead before it is heard'. It took four years for Joan to reverse the damaging decision by Para Equestrian Ireland to exclude her from its competitions. Edward likewise waited four years before his case was heard.

The fear of victimisation has to be overcome before taking a case. People can be fearful that the organisation they challenge will try to get its own back on them. Edward's case was 'nerve wracking . . . we weren't sure where we fitted into social welfare' once the case had started. Victimisation is illegal under the legislation and significant awards have been made in cases of victimisation, but it remains a concern. Mary says she 'was still fighting after the case'. She felt that nothing changed in the local authority after she won the case. 'They just got nastier.' Joan actually took a case about victimisation but she too was conscious that this could involve 'additional reprisals and further withdrawal of the voluntary services'. She still does not feel included by Para Equestrian Ireland.

The legal process can be intimidating. Sabrina felt like 'pulling the plug on the case a few times'. Joan found the Circuit Court setting for her appeal to be 'intimidating'. Mervyn and Richard were concerned that they would be outed when the case came to be heard. Phyllis noted with some awe that 'the legal team they [Ulster Bank] had must have cost a fortune.' Mary said she could get 75 per cent of the way with the case but would not have been able to finish it as she needed legal support. Edward said the hearing was 'frightening'.

Then there is the risk of failure and losing the case. Mervyn and Richard were very conscious of this. While the success of the case gave them a boost, losing the case would have been 'very demoralising'. They highlighted the personal investment made in the case and the big emotional risks involved. Joan lost her case when it was first heard in the Equality Tribunal and there was an emotional hit. It was 'terrible' and, though in her heart she felt she was right, she began to question herself. Mary felt the 'stakes were very high' because the case was personal and about her family but felt 'the fight does not end here, if I lose the case, it is for life'.

However, no regrets are expressed in these stories. Sabrina feels the experience 'made me a stronger person'. She found the hearing of the case to be both 'liberating and empowering'. Mary too highlights the importance of the hearing. She was allowed to 'say how it is' and to see the 'people who had blocked her having to sit and answer for their lies'. Mervyn and Richard found the experience gave them new confidence, has 're-awakened their interest in rights issues' and has given them new energy to engage with equality issues. Phyllis says the case 'helped her get through what she is going through' in trying to support her husband in long-term care. Joan just says 'there were better times before Para Equestrian Ireland'. Edward communicates a pride in what was achieved by his case in breaking up the segregation of Travellers in Castle Street.

The Equality Authority played a support role in all these stories. People found very different routes to it. Directory enquiries assisted Sabrina; a friend pointed Joan in the right direction; Age and Opportunity helped Phyllis and the Irish Traveller Movement helped Edward. In most cases the media profile of the Equality Authority and the equality legislation was important in ensuring people knew where to go.

The legal services of the Equality Authority were availed of to good effect in these cases. However, it is clear from the stories that a wider range of supports is needed. The technical legal support is crucial but there is also a need for social and emotional support. The comments made about the Equality Authority staff in these stories are telling in this regard. Sabrina valued 'the moral support' from her solicitor. Mervyn and Richard found the staff of the Equality Authority 'professional and helpful' but also emphasised how they were 'sympathetic and pleasant'.

Friends, family, trade unions and community groups provided important moral, practical and legal support. Joan's friend Deirdre supported her through the case. Sabrina's father came with her to Dublin each time she had to go for the case. Age and Opportunity told Phyllis where to go and what to do. Edward and his wife Winnie operated as a team in the case that Edward took. But some family and friends encouraged caution, caught up in a culture that is unsupportive of questioning and challenging the powerful. Some non-governmental organisations approached were found to be 'useless'.

The effectiveness of the equality legislation depends on people like Sabrina, Mary, Phyllis, Mervyn and Richard, Joan, Edward and Winnie. It needs courageous people to take cases when they experience discrimination. If people don't take cases, the legislation will not serve to eliminate the high levels of discrimination in Ireland. This makes a big demand on people from groups already disadvantaged by inequality and discrimination. It is important therefore to invest in and further develop the diverse range of supports needed by people taking cases.

The next chapter examines the crucial role in advancing equality played by a number of individuals—leaders, advocates, catalysts—promoting change within various organisations throughout the country.

3. Tales of organisational change

Equality requires change: in people's attitudes, in the policies and practices of organisations and in the culture and values of society. Change that seeks to achieve equality in an organisation has a central contribution to make. It improves the situation of clients and employees from groups experiencing inequality, it influences supportive staff attitudes to equality and diversity and it enables the organisation to play a leadership role on equality within its particular sector or local community.

People who champion equality within their organisations make a key contribution towards a more equal society. Such people can play a variety of roles in their organisations. They can be advocates who are given a brief to promote equality or who have simply decided to take on this role. They can be leaders who have a position of formal authority in the organisation and who choose to use that authority to promote equality within their organisations. They can be catalysts who seek to feed the process of change within their organisations by creating networks for equality or by using their position to place equality on the agenda of the different sections of their organisation. Advocates, leaders, and catalysts are all inspired by the challenge to improve their organisations, to make them better places for people and to give practical expression to the value of equality.

The following tales of change introduce some of these leaders, advocates and catalysts. They explore the source of their passion for equality, their creativity and determination and the strategies they each brought to bear in their organisation. These stories should assist in identifying what needs to be done to create the conditions for more such leaders, advocates and catalysts to emerge.

Siobhán Bigley

Siobhán Bigley is a leader. She is chief executive of Athlone Chamber of Commerce. Her first motivation in taking on equality issues was 'to help businesses. The Chamber could provide good information to business on equality issues and practices. Many local companies are small and don't have human resource people. We could fill a gap with this information.' There was a wider motivation: to 'brand Athlone as an area committed to equality, as a place of good employers and as a town where different nationalities were welcome'. This is important for business. 'An increased population was needed for Athlone to be a gateway town. Many companies depend on migrant employees. We have many businesses set up by migrant people.' The equality brand for Athlone would serve to sustain this valuable migrant presence. In addition, migrants contribute a wider benefit to Athlone in that 'diversity brings new life into the place, it brings in new things and makes a buzz'.

Siobhán's interest in equality has both family and personal origins. She remembers that her 'dad was heavily involved in social justice issues. There wasn't an organisation he wasn't involved in. The whole family have an over developed sense of justice.' Her experience 'as a woman working in a male-dominated world' is another influence. 'When I was pregnant and had my son, I had a hell of a battle as my employer pushed to get rid of me.' In the world of business 'it is men who are on the boards and only a few women are coming through. It is nearly always men who chair things, there are few women there at senior level.' She says that she is 'known as a pain for always bringing up the subject. Maybe sometimes I would have been better off not to.'

When Westmeath EQUAL, a local European-funded

project to support equality in the labour market, was try-ing to build relationships with employers. Siobhán 'felt I could do something about it'. There 'was no great interest among my board at the time. They were a bit watery about the issue.'She brought in a consultant, Andy Pearse, to run some training courses as part of the EQUAL initiative.

When funding for the EQUAL programme finished Andy put Siobhán in contact with the Equality Authority. Although she 'knew the Equality Authority' it was 'not in a very favourable light. They seemed to be out to get employ-ers. There seemed to be a wide gap as they never appeared to be helping employers.' So there was a need for a leap of trust. The Authority provided funding for a programme to help employers in Athlone to be planned and systematic in their approach to equality and to build a brand for Athlone as a town of equality. Siobhán set up a steering commit-tee to develop the programme but her board 'was still not with me. One member did put his name down for the steer-ing committee and that allowed me to do the work.' The committee had a broad membership drawn from local companies, trade unions, the local college and community organisations.

Siobhán remembers their first meeting as 'the weirdest meeting. We were all talking different languages. People were getting frustrated. It was all over the place.' This steer-ing committee eventually emerged as an important factor in the success of the programme. 'They all had their own perspectives but they were prepared to share them in a very honest way. They would thrash things out from these different perspectives and identify useful ways to move the work forward.'

Andy Pearse worked with Siobhán on this programme. A number of companies were supported to put equality pol-icies in place. They then formed a network to share experi-ences and ideas on promoting equality in their businesses.

They developed new and positive perspectives on equality in their organisations. 'So, many now see it in a very different way. They see that when you put good things into your practice there is no need to go near the Equality Tribunal. They have gone over and above the legal requirements. They have even begun to scorn other employers who don't do this.'

The high point for Siobhán lay in 'the positive response of businesses. Far more than expected got involved. Businesses were interested in the subject. They responded and came to the launch of the programme and to the various events.' This was important on a personal level given that her board was not initially supportive. It was also important because in a small town there is a greater level of personal investment in such work. 'There is a lot of personal contact in getting things going. People get involved on the basis of personal relationships. It is about them going along with you, coming in on the basis of your relationship with them. It is a high risk if it doesn't work out then because you are trading on your personal relationships.'

There were barriers to overcome. At the start 'equality was seen as a luxury. People didn't know the language.' Many on her board saw equality 'as a thorn in their side'. They were nervous about impositions from Dublin. Siobhán remembers that when she proposed to organise an event to promote work-life balance, one member of her board responded dismissively 'that's the stuff that goes on in Dublin'.

Siobhán says that the support from the Equality Authority was important. However, due to the budget cutbacks in 2009 the funding from the Authority was stopped and Siobhán no longer had the resources to keep Andy Pearse involved. The steering committee 'was reeling and the programme lost momentum'. She had another five companies lined up but could not provide the consultancy support they needed. Nonetheless, she is determined and is 'still working away and the momentum has built up again. However, it's on my own.'

Pat Normanly

Pat Normanly is an advocate. She was the first equality and diversity officer in Dublin Bus, a post established in 2001 to ensure compliance with the new equality legislation. Her brief was to establish and develop an equality and diversity programme for the company. The human resources man-ager had identified a number of challenges such as the low numbers of women going for promotion, an increasing cul-tural diversity amongst staff and the need to accommodate employees with disabilities and those with family respon-sibilities. Pat points out that 'Dublin Bus was already doing a lot of good work in this area, but did not always get credit for it, as this work was not formalised'.

She was attracted to the new job as it 'gave me an op-portunity to be involved in bringing about change, change that would be of benefit to the organisation and that would make it a better place for customers and employees.' Pat has worked in Dublin Bus for a long time. She remembers 'when women couldn't work as bus drivers, when the mar-riage bar excluded women who were married, and when almost everyone working in Dublin Bus was Dublin born. Looking back it was inclined to be stale and hierarchical. Dublin Bus now has a great diversity of employees and this diversity has been good for everyone.'

She points to the importance of advocacy. 'Dublin Bus, as the provider of a public service, has a strong social inclu-sion role. We have to constantly search for opportunities to fulfill this role.' There is a particular and defined space for effective advocacy in any organisation. She 'knew the organisation did not want someone to go off doing very radical things. They had to trust that I would operate within guidelines and that any activities would contribute to the successful operation of the business. The space has its boundaries but once you build trust more is possible.' There are dangers that the advocate may become a lone and token voice in an organisation. She was challenged 'to move it away from being just me. I had to get ownership for equality in different places, an ownership that people could relate to their different roles and functions.'

Pat was previously an administrative officer in the finance department in Dublin Bus. At first sight this seems an unusual starting point for an equality advocate. However, she also has a long experience of working in voluntary organisations on social justice issues, and was chairperson of the Dublin Simon Community. It is this commitment to social justice that has enabled her to bring to her job 'an awareness of how people are excluded, how people don't get into employment or don't progress their careers, and where the barriers are for marginalised people'. A management development course in the Irish Management Institute made her realise she 'could be using her skills from outside of work within Dublin Bus' and led her to apply for the post of equality and diversity officer. Her previous work in financial control has also assisted. She emphasises the importance in her job of gathering data on equality and diversity in the organisation, keeping this data up to date and monitoring imbalances between different groups in the workforce. She points out that she 'had experience of statistical analysis in the finance area and this has turned out to be very useful'.

Pat emphasises the need for a planned and systematic approach. An early initiative was an equality review of the situation of the diversity of staff within the organisation. The data gathered provided a foundation for the ongoing work on equality and diversity and keeping this data up to date became a key part of Pat's approach. A range of equality policies was put in place covering 'Dignity and Respect', 'Transport for All', 'Recruitment and Selection' and 'Work Life Balance'.

The high point for Pat was the preparation of an equality and diversity strategy. This 'developed objectives for Dublin Bus and did so in a language relevant to Dublin Bus. The strategy was based on Dublin Bus values of safety, efficiency, courtesy and quality. The strategy provided the mandate to bring an equality focus into all business functions—engineering, operations, finance, business development and human resources.' Equality and diversity training for managers and supervisors is an important element in implementing the strategy.

Pat is also clear that 'you have to be flexible. The organisation is changing all the time. If you don't adapt you won't progress. You need to keep an eye out for windows of opportunity.' The company is currently involved in an extensive network review project. Pat seized the opportunity to include equality impact assessments as part of the review. As each route is examined, any related equality issues are identified and addressed as a formal part of this examination. This has provided a launching pad for the next stage of her work. She says 'the focus of our strategy is now on mainstreaming. This means building a focus on equality and diversity into general policies. It is about identifying the areas where an equality impact assessment approach is relevant and practical.'

Dublin Bus was selected by the European Commission as an example of good practice in diversity management— the only Irish company to be chosen. This was an important recognition of the work being done by Pat. An award of this type is valuable in sustaining commitment in the organisation to equality and diversity. Pat identifies supportive senior management who had a good understanding of equality and shared some of the values associated with it as a key factor in the success of her work. The informal and non-hierarchical nature of the organisation also helped. The 'fact of having an Equality Authority there' was also important. She notes that 'the Equality Authority provided guidance, gave profile to the issue of equality and gave the work on equality the language it required.' She points out that 'it was important to people in the organisation that the Equality Authority recognised and valued the work that was being done in Dublin Bus.'

The Road Safety Authority's requirement for annual training for bus drivers, for their Certificate of Professional Competence, has provided a useful external stimulus for Dublin Bus to sustain its work on equality and diversity. The training includes a focus on interacting with the customer and with specific groups of customers. Dublin Bus has used this framework to develop a training module that includes a focus on the Equal Status Act and on the Dublin Bus equality policy in this area. There is a particular emphasis on disability awareness and cultural competency in the training.

Pat knows that progress can be slow but 'I'm more resigned to that now. In the beginning I would have been inclined to take on too much. Now I'm more realistic.' She remains optimistic about equality and diversity in Dublin Bus despite the economic recession. This is because 'in the end equality and diversity are about very practical things — employment policies and practices, consultation with employees and customers and the equality impact assessment approach. We have made huge strides in these areas and the values and policies we have developed are now part of everyday practice.' However, 'there remains the need for equality and diversity champions within the organisation to ensure policies and practices are implemented, to continue to promote good practice and to ensure policies and practices are relevant and effective in times of change.' Pat is now employee development and equality manager in Dublin Bus.

Shira Mehlman

Shira Mehlman is an advocate. She was the first director of social inclusion in FÁS, and held the position for five years. She says 'I do what I do because, fundamentally, I am an advocate. I want to shift mindsets about equality and about difference. It comes from my roots. I know what it can be like to experience prejudice and discrimination.' She points out that the shift in thinking required is 'ultimately about the people who receive the service. It is about them receiving a better service and it is about them being involved in the service by defining their own needs'. A related driving force for Shira is her understanding that 'public services need to show impact'.

Shira is conscious of the specific space for advocacy in a public service organisation. 'To promote an equality framework within any organisation you need to start from where the organisation is at and then push it up a notch. It is not about going the whole hog. You have to use those leverage points that the organisation has to offer in the first instance. This means you can't approach people in the organisation as the expert and tell them what to do. You have to go in and work with people and their perspectives.'

She admits that 'there are a couple of things I might have stretched too far' and suggests that advocates need to 'be able to see things from a lot of different perspectives.' She identifies consultation as 'the fundamental premise' required 'to map the terrain for change, to establish the issues, to understand the barriers people face, and to identify leverage points.' She adds that 'you have to be willing to listen to critics and understand their concerns as well as those people who agree with what you are doing.'

Shira has 'a systems focus' and says her key skill is

'understanding systems very quickly'. She says that 'organisational change is what gets me going'. A master's course in management at the Irish Management Institute fuelled her understanding of organisational development and organisational change.

Shira points to a range of influences that have shaped her commitment to equality and inclusion. 'Equality is a family profession. My mother was a learning disability consultant and my father was a strong labour advocate, as well as a university professor and psychologist.' Her grandmother was awarded a scholarship to Columbia University in New York but her 'father would not let her go because she was a woman. She was a very strong woman and in later life she was an entrepreneur, having built up several successful businesses. Yet she felt she always had to fight harder because she was a woman.' She points also to her own experience of anti-semitism. For these reasons 'the need for equality and the need to move the agenda forward are engrained in who I am.'

Shira also has a long track record of work on disability issues. In the USA she did volunteer work with children who had mental health problems and who were institutionalised in secondary school. She ran a residential home for adults with intellectual disabilities while she worked her way through university. When she came to Ireland she worked in the National Rehabilitation Board on standards for training of people with disabilities. In 2000 she started working in FÁS, as manager of the disability policy and development unit, following the Government decision to mainstream services to people with disabilities. When the post of director of social inclusion came up she knew it was what she wanted.

Shira took up her post in what was 'a changing environment for FÁS'. The increase in migrant workers, new responsibilities for people with disabilities and new labour market policies targeting lone parents all helped to put equality on the agenda. The equality legislation was also an important stimulus as 'staff were fearful of the legislation'. She points out that 'FÁS was doing a lot already. What was needed was a comprehensive perspective across all parts of the organisation. We needed to move from a range of disparate activities to a focus on strategy, outcomes and impact on particular groups of people.'

The development of an equality policy for customers was a key achievement in her work. This involved 'elaborate consultation with people from across the nine grounds covered by the equality legislation and within the organisation. I talked with management groups and partnership groups across all divisions of FÁS. At any large conclave within the organisation I would just put it on the agenda.' One example she gives is of using the board's interest in disability as a leverage point to successfully recommend that the board set up a sub-committee on social inclusion.

The equality policy commits FÁS to ensuring diversity is taken into account in the services it provides. This is done by discussing individual customers' needs with them and by consulting organisations representing groups experiencing inequality about the adjustments they need in the service provided. The policy makes the promotion of equality a requirement in all contracts. Organisations providing services to FÁS have to give evidence of their equality policies and practices. The policy also promotes positive action to facilitate participation by all groups in general FÁS programmes.

The policy was published in 2006. This allowed Shira to 'sell a vision. When I saw how all the pieces could fit together I had my organisational change programme.' Equality and diversity training for all staff, and equality proofing to ensure the assessment of the equality impact of all actions planned or taken, are key supports to implementation.

These are the drivers for organisational change.

For the future she emphasises the 'need to embed equality proofing and make it part of day to day business in all divisions'. Equality proofing is a system for assessing the impact of new policies and programmes on groups experiencing inequality. An equality group will be established at national level in the organisation to equality proof every new policy.

At the start Shira felt that 'FÁS didn't know what social inclusion was' and that it was important to 'increase the exposure of people by bringing the voice of people experiencing inequality into the institutional process'. She was helped by having 'a strong advocate for equality above me' at assistant director general level. She says that 'without this support it would have been a very difficult sell within the organisation'. She adds that the 'work was done by very few staff. It was not costly around resources though it did take time.' It is important that the approach 'is fluid. We changed our path as the times changed around us. We did not follow a step by step approach. We seized opportunities as they arose.' She goes further in stressing that 'you need to be comfortable with ambiguity and chaos. It does not matter where you start or whether it fits into a preconceived linear plan. Eventually, working through multiple levels, the influences will permeate every level.'

Shira worked with the Further Education and Training Awards Council (FETAC) and the Equality Authority on the development of the equality elements in FETAC policy guidelines for providers of further education and training such as FÁS. FETAC requires providers to make equality training available to their staff and to have an equality action plan based on an audit of their current provision from an equality perspective (*Quality Assurance on Further Education and Training—Policy and Guidelines for Providers*, FETAC). Shira points out that 'it was crucial to build these requirements into the FETAC policy guidelines. Building equality into another "regulatory instrument" meant that equality was not seen in isolation. Since this is something that was going to affect the core business of FÁS, it moved it up the organisational agenda. It was no longer something that was being promoted by a small unit within the organisation. It was part of what we had to do to ensure our training had currency. This was crucial for the sustainability of our work on equality.'

With high rates of unemployment Shira is concerned that 'the equality policy and social inclusion will go off the agenda. The focus will be on the numbers coming through, rather than diversity and equality. Yet our raison d'etre should include social inclusion alongside other priorities. Fundamentally, public services are about providing services to those whose needs are not being met by the market.' She also notes that the emergence of the recession will mean fewer programmes targeted on specific groups. This could mean 'we have a more equality enabled organisation' to ensure people from these groups can and do participate in the general programmes. There will 'now be a challenge to build the power of the centre to achieve equality enablement'.

Jack Keyes

Jack Keyes is a leader. He is county manager in Cavan. He focuses on 'employee colleagues, citizens served by the local authority and other organisations in the local delivery landscape'. An important starting point is respect: 'If people treat people with respect, then the analysis develops and vice versa'. He looks to a future where he sees that 'local government will be more and more about quality of life, inclusion and equality, and less about the technical matters of roads or water'. These are the foundations of his concern for equality within the organisation.

He is thoughtful about the nature of leadership. He says that in his position 'you have an amount of power, you can push boundaries out and you can take risks'. But there are limitations. 'I have formal authority. I could get people to do things about equality. But you need to get people to buy into it, or they will just revert back to a traditional way of doing things.' He says that 'the equality legislation was an important factor in giving legitimacy to a leadership for equality within the organisation'.

Jack replaced someone with a very different approach to the job of county manager and notes that 'I could not come in with a new broom. I started slowly.' He 'would lose support if I became an outspoken advocate'. He differentiates his role as leader from that of advocates who 'see a problem, come to the system with a solution and continue to push for its implementation'. In his position he 'must continually build alliances and consensus around a variety of issues'. He quotes Eisenhower who said that 'the only power I have is the power to persuade'. He defines his role as leader as seeking to achieve 'success through persuasion, passion and providing direction'. In exploring how to bring about organisational change he notes that 'the technical solutions are easy but much more difficult are the people issues and complex areas such as social exclusion'.

He sees the need for advocates in the county council. Leaders can 'use their formal authority to create the conditions for things to happen' and he has worked to create the conditions for the emergence of more advocates for equality within the organisation. However, he acknowledges that 'this can be a difficult role in a hierarchical organisation as, traditionally, you didn't succeed by being an advocate'. He adds that 'my role is to make it safe for people to become empowered while still focusing on the short-term demands of their posts'.

Jack is a civil engineer by training and was senior

executive engineer and later director of community and enterprise in Offaly County Council. Senior executive engineer would appear to be an unpromising starting point for a leader on equality issues given its technical emphasis and the stereotypes that surround engineers. Growing up in Athy, in a corner shop, he had early exposure to poverty and social exclusion. He remembers 'doing deliveries during the fifties and sixties into houses that had no bathrooms'. He remembers going to the local Christian Brothers school where 'many guys from one side of town left school at fourteen and went to England or ended up in prison, though they were good people'.

He recalls that in 'sixty eight I was swept along convinced that the world was going to change'. At college he was involved in student politics as a member of the student council. He also had an interest in Third World issues and saw civil engineering as playing a fundamental role in providing infrastructure in the developing world. All of this had an influence. When he met his partner, Julie Smyth, in 1988 he was re-exposed to poverty and exclusion through her involvement in the Clondalkin Travellers Development Group. A master's course in public management in the Institute of Public Administration also helped his 'mind get freed up to see the limitations to the technical solutions and the necessity to tap into my own potential to create change'.

The break with his background as a civil engineer came when he applied for the new post of director of community and enterprise in Offaly County Council. He worked to a county development board which was responsible for preparing and implementing a ten-year strategy for economic, social and cultural development in the county. The board had a particular focus on counteracting social exclusion. The post involved promotion which was attractive, and by this time Jack had also become 'interested in making an impact on social inclusion and could see the limitations in being county engineer in so far as decision making involved political work—with a small and large P'. He was later appointed county manager in Cavan County Council.

People with disabilities were the initial focus in the work on equality in Cavan County Council. The Equality Authority supported an initiative to provide training for staff on equality and disability issues. This helped staff to identify and pursue actions in each part of the organisation to improve access for people with disabilities. Jack notes that 'the focus on disability was needed but it was also a relatively safe starting point. People could start talking about inclusion and equality around people with disability. It was not a huge step to transfer this across to other more difficult grounds.' A committee was formed to progress this work. It was named Creating Reasonable Accommodation In Cavan—the CRAIC team. This work has been expanded through other cross departmental teams working with young people, lone parents and other target groups. Work is also currently underway on examining the issue of gender imbalance in senior local government jobs. A social inclusion strategy will provide the framework for future action.

Another key step in the work was to commission an employment equality review of the organisation, again with support from the Equality Authority. This looked at the staff equality situation across the nine grounds and reviewed all policies and procedures for their impact on equality for these staff. This was an important step in putting equality on the agenda and in charting a way forward. It also served to make equality one of the factors driving a wider modernisation of the organisation.However, 'while doing the review was important, there was resistance. It took a long time to get it to happen. You have to quietly persevere.' In the end there were 'a lot of positives in the review compared to other local authorities and progress has been made'.

The focus for all this work was 'on the way we do business. In this, attitudes are key and training on equality is important.' Staff training on specific equality issues was provided and equality modules were included in other training courses. The high points for Jack in this work are tied up in this emphasis on attitudinal change. He points to moments where 'at the end of a project a staff member makes a presentation and says something very powerful. This has happened in all the projects.' He talks of 'one to one conversations with staff and seeing the analysis coming through'. It is a slow process promoting equality, but in the end it is about 'the way people think, understand and analyse'. These are the markers of success and you 'achieve this success through persuasion and through local relationships'.

In parallel with this, change is driven through new policy formation, 'much of which can be driven from the top of the organisation, to make it all work. The final piece of the jigsaw is the re-orientation of systems and structures.' He also emphasises that 'the support of local politicians has been remarkable. Most are driven by a desire to improve people's conditions.' According to Jack: 'The democratic legitimacy of local government is fundamental.'

He points to external factors that contributed to the success of this work such as the Local Government Act 2001 which gave local authorities 'a fundamental role to promote social inclusion and a leadership role in the local development landscape. This was crucial in legitimising and driving this type of work.' The Combat Poverty Agency has contributed hugely through its work in support of local government in this area. The influence of the Local Government Management Services Board was important, particularly their support for staff training and for disability access. Jack says that 'the Equality Authority usefully strengthened this connection with the Local Government Management Services Board in the face of some initial resistance'.

The economic recession is a barrier to this work. 'This is a potentially unhealthy moment for equality. If you look at the language currently being used in the system, it is about getting back to basics—to the more technical issues of water and roads.' He emphasises that 'equality and social inclusion don't take a lot of money, small amounts can make a huge difference'. Jack notes that 'people are scared by change and they draw back into themselves. They look for securities that will carry them through. It is the same with systems.' Leaders need to hold steady and persevere. He also points out 'that everyone is getting more work thrown at them. It is things like the CRAIC meetings that can then be let go under the pressure. There are dangers in this, as equality can go off the agenda. But you can't go back.'

Bride Rosney

Bride Rosney is a catalyst. Until recently she was director of communications at RTÉ, a post that included a coordinating role at the heart of its various business divisions. While it was not in her brief, Bride took on the challenges of interculturalism. She felt that 'RTÉ had been addressing the issue of cultural diversity, but not very satisfactorily. It was essentially a box-ticking exercise. We had *Mono* and other individual programmes. However, there was no mainstreaming across all programming. Cultural diversity was not visible in audiences or expert panels, for example.'

She identified the need for a coordinated policy across television and radio. The role of catalyst was 'about building a critical mass of people behind the project' to develop an intercultural policy for RTÉ and to implement this policy through an annual action plan. She worked with colleagues and 'an ad hoc group from across the integrated business divisions in RTÉ'. To achieve an intercultural approach, she says, 'it was essential to get people to grasp hold of it, especially in programmes, and to lead on it'. She says, by way of example, that the role of Clare Duignan, then director of television programmes, was hugely important. 'She took it on board very quickly and set enormous objectives for TV.' The catalyst's role was about 'putting it on the agenda. You can't issue diktats. You have to build acceptance and make it clear that the issue was not going away.' The approach was 'a slow burner. Don't do it in a way that will alienate people. Turn up the gas tap as best you can.'

Bride has an impressive background in issues of equality and human rights. She was special advisor to Mary Robinson when she was President of Ireland and later United Nations High Commissioner for Human Rights. She points to earlier formative influences for her commitment to equality. She remembers lying on the floor as a six- or seven-year-old reading a newspaper article about a court case in Cork. A man was suing his neighbor for compensation for having an affair with his wife. He won his case on the grounds that the wife was merely 'a chattel of her husband'. She asked her father what a chattel was. He got her to look it up in the dictionary. Equality was born as an issue for her when she found that chattel meant that the woman was part of the man's belongings— 'like pots and pans'. She asked her father if her mother was a chattel. He explained the difference between law and justice.

She also had an early exposure to socio-economic injustice. Her first job as a teacher was in Ballyfermot. She can remember the concern of her friends when they heard where she was going to work but says that 'it was the best job I have ever had'. It made her see, first-hand, the economic pressure on the young girls forced out of school to work by the age of fifteen. Later she worked as a teacher with visually impaired children.

At different stages of her career she was exposed to various aspects of diversity. She vividly remembers an occasion when she was working in Geneva with Mary Robinson. A Nigerian official came into her office to break some bad news. Bride put her head in her hands saying, 'I don't believe you' as a mark of her distress. The Nigerian official took umbrage and reported her to senior authorities for calling him a liar. This expanded her understanding of the challenges posed in managing cultural diversity effectively.

Bride advanced her work on the intercultural policy on the basis of RTÉ's 2006 corporate social responsibility report. This 'provided the framework as it acknowledged RTE's responsibilities to a wide range of major stakeholders including an audience that was intercultural.' The way forward on the policy was 'eased because everyone knew it was a critical challenge for RTÉ'. The first challenge was 'to establish what the issue was. The multicultural approach was already discredited at the BBC. The multi-cultural approach can dilute everything to a lowest common denominator. We came to the issue on the basis of an intercultural approach. This focuses on the challenge of people from different cultures living together.'

The intercultural policy statement and action plan were agreed by RTÉ in 2007. This was 'a short sharp statement of policy. RTÉ has done many and worthy policies but in some cases they just sat on a shelf. The accompanying annual action plan was key.' In it 'we decided to focus on mainstreaming cultural diversity across all areas rather than keeping it in its own cubbyhole. We also decided to focus on cultural diversity in staff training and recruitment.' She points to the audience council as 'a useful sounding board for this initiative. They are pretty representative of a comprehensive sweep of groups and include people who applied to be on it.' The Equality Authority was a member of the audience council.

Getting the policy and action plan into print was a high point for Bride. It meant RTÉ now 'had definite measurable objectives on interculturalism. They had requirements to account for these within a year. RTÉ takes accountability and transparency seriously.' A solid foundation for action had been achieved. She emphasises that this 'was not a regulatory requirement. It was self imposed. It is a lot less desireable if it is regulatory as you just end up with a tick box exercise.'

The 2008 corporate social responsibility report 'had a big objective around human resources'. This allowed intercultural training to be developed and provided to staff, first at induction training and then across the integrated business divisions. 'We needed a new mindset and awareness. The training will help to stoke this new mindset.'

The European Union provided 'a useful framework' for the work—2007 was the European Year of Equal Opportunities for All; and 2008 was the European Year of Intercultural Dialogue. RTÉ, through Bride, got involved in the Irish action programmes for each year. She 'wanted interculturalism to become more of a norm as a culmination of the two years'. She also wanted to demonstrate that this 'could be done at no cost'. During 2008 'we did a hell of a lot. Every main daytime show that went out had an intercultural presence.' However, 'RTÉ was somewhat isolated and wondered whether other corporates in Ireland were doing anything significant on the issue.'

It was not all plain sailing within RTÉ either. There was inevitably some resistance. 'Not everyone believed it was necessary. It is about change and there is resistance to change. It is a passive resistance based on the notion that "we are doing fine". There is no evidence it was an anti-equality resistance.' In this context 'it was important to see the process as small bites taken on an ongoing basis so as to address this resistance to change.'

Bride is interested to see what happens now. When there is a recession she fears that 'money can be a great excuse' for inaction. Overall she is optimistic that 'the things already happening in RTÉ will be fine. The key is mindset and mainstreaming interculturalism across all programmes. It is often only the more imaginative stuff that does take money.'

Dorinda Ryder

Dorinda Ryder is an advocate. She is a senior human resource generalist in Medtronic, a global medical technology company with a facility in Galway. She joined the company in 2005 and managing employee relations is her major function. In 2006 the company decided they needed to streamline their various diversity initiatives into a single strategy. Dorinda volunteered to take on this project. She says 'this is a topic you have to be passionate about. There is no point putting someone into this type of role who has no interest in it, as it requires personal commitment. It is never just a job.'

Dorinda says diversity is 'something I was always interested in'. She did her masters in human resources in NUI Galway and wrote her thesis on migrant workers. She used the Equality Authority website during her course. The equality legislation provides a framework for her work. 'It is your base and you work from there. You write your policies around it. There are other factors, but legislation is the number one influence.' Dorinda's work seeks 'to create and sustain an inclusive environment for all employees and to create an awareness of all areas of diversity across the nine grounds'. A key goal for her is 'to tie this focus on diversity into all our employment processes including recruitment, performance reviews, talent management, development planning and succession planning'. She strives for a workplace where 'human differences are explored and valued'.

As an advocate for diversity and inclusion, a key part of Dorinda's work 'is to continue to bring these issues to the senior management team so as to make sure targets are met'. This is 'not always easy as things can come up and diversity and inclusion can be moved down the priority list. My job is to make sure that does not happen.'

A key pressure initially was the rapid growth in the cultural diversity of employees in the company. In early 2006, 26 different nationalities were represented on the staff in the Galway facility and this has since grown to 41. This provided a starting point for Dorinda's work. An intercultural awareness week was organised and was well received by employees. The week 'was a very popular initiative. People wanted to get involved in it. It helped decrease any employee relations issues that might have come with this increase in cultural diversity.' A later initiative was a disability awareness day. This included hosting a stand from People With Disabilities Ireland in the staff canteen. There were 'mixed feelings regarding this event. Some people found it difficult to see what we were trying to achieve.' This captured 'the fine line between raising awareness whilst trying not to cause upset'. However, 'we have employees with disabilities and as a company we need to make people aware that you can disclose your disability and that there are supports in place for employees with disabilities.'

Dorinda's core work involved examining company policies and processes 'to see if they made reference to equality and were in compliance with the law'. Although relevant policies made reference to equality there was no diversity statement so one was prepared. Next up was training. 'The Office of Workplace Inclusion in our Minneapolis headquarters had a training programme called "Maximising Performance through Inclusion". We were able to tailor this to Irish law and Irish culture. It was great to have this resource.' Training was provided for senior management, the diversity and inclusion council, the human resources group and then all staff on the site.

The diversity and inclusion council was another important development. It involves staff from different functions and departments and it has helped to move topics of diversity and inclusion beyond human resources. Each year it is chaired by a member of senior management. Another development was the organisation of staff focus groups on gender and on disability. These initiatives allow the company to see what staff are thinking about the topic being focused on and what needs to be done in this area.

Dorinda looked to IBEC for support. 'I spoke to IBEC and used a diversity model they had.' She was aware of the Equality Authority but 'I didn't use the Equality Authority. I would see it as a resource for employees where they can get support and information on equal rights in employment.' Headquarters in Minneapolis was a source of valuable support. 'I am in regular contact with the office of workplace inclusion. They have trained diversity and inclusion professionals who have worked in this area for many years.'

Headquarters in Minneapolis drives the diversity and inclusion agenda. But Dorinda points out that 'we also have choices in Galway about what we do in this area. Also if headquarters was not there we would continue to do this work. We have a lot of people who are passionate about it.' She notes that senior management support was important to the success of the work. 'They are prepared to give us resources and to give us a voice at the senior management table which shows the importance of the issues.'

'Medtronic in Galway is an operational site and staff can find it challenging to get involved in activities without compromising operations. But employees do take time in and around their shifts.' It can be hard to keep the momentum going. 'Of course there is a small percentage of people who don't see the value of having such a programme in these times. However, I see it as even more important if we want to keep our best people. That is why it is important to share the business case for diversity.' The fact that diversity and inclusion are identified as a main goal in all cardio vascular facilities of the company across the world 'helps sustain the work and keeps diversity and inclusion to the top of the agenda'.

Leaders, advocates and catalysts stimulate and drive change in their organisations. They seek to ensure that their organisations can more effectively promote equality, manage diversity and eliminate discrimination. These tales of change show that this organisational change has a range of goals. Ultimately it is about improving the experience of customers and employees from across the nine grounds. It is also about making organisations better at what they do.

Bride Rosney wanted RTE to respond better to the critical challenge of an intercultural audience. Pat Normanly wanted Dublin Bus to be a better place for customers and employees as well as being a more effective business. Siobhán Bigley developed Athlone Chamber of Commerce as a support to local companies to respond to their obligations under equality legislation. She also wants to enable Athlone to attract and benefit from a diversity of people living and working there. Jack Keyes wants to shape how business is done in Cavan County Council and to place respect for people at the heart of business relationships. Dorinda Ryder seeks to create a working environment in Medtronic that is inclusive of a diversity of employees. Shira Mehlman aimed to ensure FÁS provided a better service to people and enabled them to define their own needs and how these needs should be responded to.

To be a leader, advocate or catalyst for equality is not just a job. As Dorinda says, it is work that needs to be informed by passion. These tales of change are about people who brought passion to their work on equality and diversity. Their commitment had different sources--family, personal experience and involvements outside the workplace formed the value base that informs this work. It is clear from Pat though, that it can be necessary to convince people to draw from these sources outside the workplace, so that they can make their full contribution to equality in their organisations.

These different roles of leader, advocate and catalyst are vital if organisations are to promote equality for employees and customers and if organisations are to benefit from this commitment to equality. If people do not come forward to play these roles, or if organisations do not provide a mandate for these roles, the necessary organisational change will not be achieved. Although organisations may take specific equality initiatives they will fail to develop these into an effective and sustained strategy for equality without leaders, advocates or catalysts for equality.

Bride talks about the importance of building a critical mass behind RTE's intercultural policy and action plan. Pat highlights the need to promote good practice, to support the implementation of equality and diversity policies and to ensure that these policies are relevant and effective in times of change. Dorinda notes the need to remind senior management of their commitments and targets in this area. Shira emphasises the challenge to shift mindsets about equality as a key foundation for change. Jack points to the quiet perseverance needed to maintain momentum on the issues. Siobhán says that local businesses were interested in equality but that there was no one doing anything about it.

Systems change is at the heart of these different tales of change. The preparation of equality policies or diversity statements, the provision of equality and diversity training to staff, the implementation of equality reviews of policies and procedures and the development of equality action plans and strategies are the key actions taken in the different organisations. These actions ensure a planned and systematic approach to equality in the organisation. Mainstreaming is identified as the core driver for systems change. Dorinda seeks to tie diversity and inclusion into all employment processes. Bride emphasises the need for an intercultural focus in all programmes rather than cultural diversity having its own cubbyhole. Shira has established equality proofing as a way of making equality a part of day to day business. Pat is using equality impact assessments as a means of building equality into general policymaking in the organisation.

The equality legislation is seen as an important influence. Jack identifies it as a source of legitimacy for his leadership on equality. Pat sees it as a stimulus for the organisation to focus on equality and diversity issues. Shira notes that one driver for organisational change was staff fear of the equality legislation. Dorinda emphasises compliance with the legislation as the base around which diversity policies should be developed.

The Equality Authority is identified as playing useful support roles. It provided guidance and funding to the work. It was seen as creating a supportive context for the work by giving a profile to the issues and a language for the work. However, there are challenges: Siobhán felt she had to take a leap of trust to work with the Equality Authority and Dorinda felt it was inappropriate to engage with it.

Other external influences serve to stimulate and sustain the work of advocates, catalysts and leaders for equality. Shira notes the importance of the requirements for equality training and equality action plans in the guidance from FETAC for providers of vocational training. These requirements are valuable in helping to sustain the work on equality in FÁS. Jack highlights the provisions of the Local Government Act 2001 that made social inclusion a role for the local authorities as a crucial influence on the work of promoting equality in a local authority setting. Pat points to the requirements of the Road Safety Authority in relation to the ongoing training of bus drivers. This has underpinned ongoing training on equality issues. Bride sounds a note of warning, however, as she stresses the importance of self-imposed targets and commitments. She notes the danger that regulatory requirements could just end up as tick box exercises.

The current context poses challenges to the work of leaders, advocates and catalysts for equality. Siobhán notes the difficulties now that the funding support from the Equality Authority is no longer available. Shira points to the danger that equality and social inclusion can go off the agenda in times of economic recession. Jack describes how systems turn in on themselves in times of crisis and return to traditional basics. This could lead to a loss of focus on equality issues. He also points to the increased pressures on staff and how this can lead to a de-prioritisation of equality commitments. Bride notes that lack of money can be used as an excuse for inaction on issues of equality and diversity.

All these tales of change end on a note of confidence. Siobhán managed to build up the momentum again in the Athlone Chamber of Commerce programme of work with local businesses. Pat points out that equality and diversity are about good practice in employment and customer service. She feels equality and diversity are now strongly embedded in Dublin Bus and have become part of everyday practice. Shira suggests that the current context might even be advantageous in that possible reductions in the number of programmes targeted on particular groups will put pressure on the general training programmes to be more equality enabled. An equality group is to be established in FÁS to equality proof all new policies. Jack notes that equality and social inclusion don't take a lot of money. He sees no going back for Cavan County Council and believes that the future for local authorities will be even more about quality of life, equality and social inclusion. Bride feels that what has been put in place in RTE will persist. The process is about mindsets and mainstreaming not money. Dorinda points out that if there are barriers to further progress they will be overcome given that diversity and inclusion have been established by Medtronic as a main goal for all its cardio vascular facilities around the world.

Siobhán says that the equality initiative was damaged when the Authority's budget was cut by 43 per cent. Many people 'remarked on it. People were saying that if that is the way the Government thinks about equality, why should we bother about it? The message came out clearly that equality is not important.'

How and why this came about is dealt with in the next chapters. Over the years, we had had to defend our position against some hostile media commentators, vested interests, and—more importantly in the long run—powerful influences within the civil service and government who did not share our enthusiasm for the equality agenda; these forces, as we shall see, eventually prevailed.

4. Contesting equality

It was perhaps inevitable that there should be conflict as to how far the equality agenda should go—this is part of our democratic process. We were committed to implementing our mandate, no more and no less. When we came up against backlash we contested it. There are tales of contest to be told from each year since the Authority's establishment. Three of these are particularly significant: media backlash in 2001, conflict with the vintners in 2002 and a series of entanglements with the Department of Justice, Equality and Law Reform. These included an attempt to sack me in 2004, inclusion of the Equality Authority in the Government's decentralisation programme and a legal contest to our understanding of our powers that ended up in the Supreme Court.

Media backlash, 2001

On 25 February 2000 Ryanair advertised in *The Irish Times* for a director of regulatory affairs. It was looking for a 'young and dynamic professional'. Just to make sure prospective candidates got the point the advertisement went on to reiterate that the ideal candidate would be 'young and dynamic'. We thought Ryanair was in breach of the equality legislation by communicating an intent to discriminate against older people and we brought a case against the airline to the Equality Tribunal. Nobody over forty years of age had applied for the job. Older people had got the message. Ryanair claimed that the advertisement meant 'young in spirit' and that it was not discriminatory.

In late December 2000 the Equality Tribunal decided that Ryanair was in breach of the equality legislation and the company was ordered to pay the Authority £8,000 compensation. We gave the money to an organisation fighting ageism. Ryanair was also ordered to place a conspicuous advertisement in *The Irish Times* stating its commitment to principles of equality and to reviewing its recruitment policies. This was the first finding of age discrimination under the Employment Equality Acts.

Initial media coverage, in February 2001, was detailed and accurate, setting out the facts of the case and the Tribunal decision. Then Brendan O'Connor, in what was supposed to be a light-hearted and humorous piece in the *Sunday Independent*, set the backlash ball rolling. He said that the judgement was 'ludicrous'. He went on to address what he saw as the implications of the case by calling up images of airplane stewardesses with zimmer frames and toothless old ladies on posters in record shops (11 February 2001). We responded with a press release criticising the article for misrepresenting the problem of ageism and demeaning older people. We also criticised the editorial policy of the paper for giving free rein to journalists wishing to attack and ridicule minority groups.

A media furore was unleashed that lasted some three weeks. The Equality Authority was the focus for attack and ridicule from a group of journalists who seemed to be hunting as a pack. We were to be in their sights for the next eight years.

It was all a bit of a surprise. The week before, we had launched a research report on the disadvantages lesbian and gay couples experience in the absence of partnership rights. We thought all hell would break loose. I had received special media training to manage the predicted outcry. Not a whisper of controversy was heard. The media coverage was accurate, thoughtful and supportive. Even the *Sun* reported the findings of the report without sensation. No backlash. Days later a small case on ageism in a job advertisement exploded into controversy. Some things you can't predict.

Trivialisation of equality issues is the tool of choice for the media pundits of backlash. They also use hyperbole and inaccuracy. Kevin Myers, writing in *The Irish Times*, turned the two separate bodies involved—the Equality Authority and the Equality Tribunal—into a single, all-powerful 'Equality Council': '"Wanted: Person to Do a Job" might stand as the Equality Council's ideal advertisement', he wrote. He berated the 'egalitarian priesthood'. 'Egalitarianism is like any other religion, and its officers like any other priests. Its existence depends not on evidence of the mind, but on blind faith, and its priests invoke a higher divine authority to justify their actions. Logic and commonsense do not apply to the creed of egalitarianism' (14 February 2001). Peter Cunningham published an article in the *Irish Independent* under the title 'Age shall not wither them, but PC brigade just might'. He wrote: 'Last week all copies of *The Old Man and the Sea* were removed from the bookshelves of bookshops' and 'Hemingway's publishers have provisionally agreed to retitle the novel *The Ageless Person and the Sea*'. Oldcastle and Old Bawn, he suggested, were going to be renamed (24 February 2001). John A. Murphy, in the *Sunday Independent*, wrote that 'the law was certainly an ass in this case' and bemoaned the 'puritanical new inquisition' (18 February 2001).

In an article for *The Irish Times*, responding to Kevin Myers, I noted the speed with which he had sprung to the defence of Brendan O'Connor and suggested that 'the priesthood of free speech is both select and fragile' (20 February 2001). I wrote that free speech 'cannot be more important than mutual respect, personal dignity and societal harmony' and that 'without according a similar status to those values free speech for all is not even possible'. I called for a debate on the role of the media—a debate to explore how stereotypes could be challenged by the media, how journalists could be informed about equality issues, and how the media could contribute to equality.

A central claim by some media commentators is that equality has gone too far and must be reined back. Ruth Dudley Edwards joined the fray with an article in *The Irish Times*. She suggested that the inevitable conclusion to be drawn from my article was 'We will all have to be re-educated. By the Equality Authority'. She added: 'in today's Ireland you have to watch what you say or you'll face excommunication by the Equality Authority'. She concluded that 'The rule of the people is being replaced by the tyranny of pressure groups' (21 February 2001). Liam Collins maintained that 'Equality is a booming industry in the new Ireland' on the basis of the €5 million being spent on the Equality Authority and the Equality Tribunal (*Sunday Independent* 18 February 2001). Éilis O'Hanlon, in the same paper, wrote: 'If the Equality Agency now sees its role as a broader one of "promoting equality" in whatever way it happens to see fit, then it needs to be stressed that this was not part of its function when it was established' (18 February 2001). More inaccuracy. One of the functions of the Equality Authority is to promote equality of opportunity in the areas covered by the equality legislation.

Another claim is that equality has become a problem for society and for those experiencing inequality. Brendan O'Connor mocked: 'To hell with suitability and with talent. In this glorious age of equality everyone should get the chance to do whatever they want' (*Sunday Independent* 11 February 2001). According to Kevin Myers: 'For the most part you're not naturally disqualified from a job because of your race (though a black garda might have trouble operating undercover in Kilbarrack). But you are by sex and you are by age.' He concluded that 'only the inquisitional dogma of the new state church of egalitarianism, unsustained by logic or by evidence, but enforced by a grim and unsmiling priesthood with apparently arbitrary legal powers, insists otherwise' (*The Irish Times* 14 February 2001). John A. Murphy wrote in the *Sunday Independent:* 'I am old. But I don't need an obtrusive and misplaced political correctness being exercised on my behalf' (18 February 2001). This myth defines the promotion of equality as imposing a status quo that lacks logic or commonsense. Equality is falsely posited as an intrusion into the lives of people experiencing inequality—forcing them into roles they are not suited for and patronising them with an unwanted political correctness.

The media furore came to a head on 20 February when I was interviewed by Éamon Dunphy on *The Last Word*. Kevin Myers was an increasingly silent guest in the studio as the interview developed. Éamon was incensed by the Authority's response to Brendan O'Connor's article and by our opinions on the responsibilities of the media. His anger grew as he harangued me about satire. H. L. Mencken, Auberon Waugh and Myles na Gopaleen were all paraded before me, again and again, as he sought to establish the inadequacy of my understanding of humour. *Monty Python's Flying Circus* was last up as, almost shouting by now, he told me 'The whole idea of humour and satire, it's savage.' Hindsight, and the advice of more learned friends, pointed out that I should have then said 'Yes, Éamon, but no-one expects the Spanish Inquisition.'

I felt almost physically battered by his onslaught, so much so that I missed the significance of his crunch line— the line that ended the media furore. He said: 'We don't need fuckers like you telling us what we can do.' The next day Chris Lowry in the *Evening Herald* described the interview 'as scandalous—not in a cool anti-establishment way but in a nasty, bullying way' (21 February 2001). Éamon Dunphy had crossed a line and the pack could not follow.

That was the end of the hunt and the media coverage became more positive from then on. *The Irish Times* published a positive profile of me (24 February 2001). A thoughtful article by Terry Prone on ageism closed the debate. She wrote in the *Sunday Independent* on 25 February: 'Ireland is one of the most unashamedly ageist countries in Europe, if not the world', and 'Never mind political correctness: we're up to our armpits in gerontophobia (fear/hatred of old people)' and 'The owners of the prejudices are comfortably certain that their prejudices are fact'.

It is the fear of change that motivates backlash. It is not a response to progress made in achieving equality. Rather, it is a response to the possibility of achieving equality. It is a pre-emptive strike designed to block progress on equality issues. Dick Walsh caught this aspect of backlash in an aside in an article in *The Irish Times*. He said that he did not believe that the case taken against Ryanair amounted to an attack on free speech and 'I'm certain that the cause of free speech is not served by heaping abuse on the [chief executive officer] of the Equality Authority, Niall Crowley, as happened on Today FM's *The Last Word*. Any suggestion of the need for equality—any attempt to make this lop-sided society fairer—brings out the hysterical worst in some of our colleagues' (24 February 2001).

Backlash also aims to demobilise those who promote equality and to demonise those who seek such change. The *Sunday Independent* gave an opinion piece on the issue by Éilis O'Hanlon the headline 'A New Age of Busybodies and Pen-Pushers'. She wrote: 'The Authority has three times more staff, and four times more budget to spend than its predecessor. And the doors have probably been expanded to allow their heads to get through as well. It stands to reason that something must be found for all these jobsworths and pen-pushers to do all day' (18 February 2001). Ruth Dudley Edwards wrote in *The Irish Times* that she had 'great respect for the decency and selflessness Niall Crowley has shown during his long career of helping the underprivileged. But in his new role he frightens me' (21 February 2001).

Brendan O'Connor had the final say in *The Dubliner* in April. He caught the pack-like nature of the pundits of backlash while cloaking himself as a defender of free speech. He wrote: 'The Dublin newspaper crowd is just like one big family. Everyone hates each other and they fight all the time—scribbling rivalry they call it. Petty squabbles are put aside, however, if the family comes under threat, as Niall Crowley of the Orwellianly named Equality Authority found out when he decided to single-handedly take on freedom of speech.' He continued: 'I can't say it didn't tickle my ego to see the likes of Kevin Myers, Ruth Dudley Edwards, John A. Murphy (professor) and Éilis O' Hanlon jump to my defence.' He was particularly pleased with Éamon Dunphy: 'Most gratifying for me was the sound of Éamon Dunphy at pains to point out what a talentless twat I was while simultaneously defending me and the family against Crowley.'

I used to play table tennis with Trevor White, publisher of *The Dubliner*, although I have to admit he was way above my standard. At the time we didn't know each other well, to the point where he knew me only as 'Niall' (he pronounced it 'Nile'). I remember at one point he asked me where I worked. I told him the Equality Authority. He was immediately interested and asked me what it was like to work with Niall Crowley. My smile gave me away before this exchange could develop to even more intriguing levels.

Later in 2001, the Labour Court found a firm of solicitors in Waterford, M. M. Halley & Sons, to be in breach of the equality legislation. The firm was ordered to pay £6,000 to a woman in her fifties whom they had dismissed on the age ground. The woman, who was employed as a legal secretary, said that she had been told by one of the partners that the firm had decided to take on 'a young girl' who could be trained to do her job. There was no media furore this time. The coverage was detailed and accurate. Clearly, challenging ageism had become routine and was accepted without controversy.

The media pundits of backlash did not disappear, however; some of them were also eventually to delight in the cutbacks to our budget in 2008.

The vintners, 2002

The vintners constituted a vociferous, powerful and effective strand of opposition to the equality agenda. The leading lights were Tadg O'Sullivan, then chief executive of the Vintners Federation of Ireland, Frank Fell, then chief executive of the Licenced Vintners Association and Chris Lavelle, then chairperson of the Westport Vintners Association. The Equal Status Act, and its prohibition on discrimination in the provision of goods and services, was the target for their ire.

As soon as the Equal Status Act was enacted, in October 2000, numerous cases were taken against public houses. In our Annual Report for 2001 we noted that the 'almost overwhelming volume of cases arising [under the Equal Status Act] was unexpected and unprecedented particularly in the area of refusal of service by publicans to members of the Traveller community'. We suggested that this was indicative of 'persistent, sustained and endemic discrimination and a profound reluctance to make this arena of social interaction more inclusive'.

Tadg O'Sullivan was not one for holding back in his statements on the equality legislation and the Equality Authority. In July 2002, he declared that 'The level of intimidation and violence has multiplied thirty fold since the

Act was introduced. But there is nothing publicans can do about it now. If they refuse to serve Travellers now they can be hauled up in front of "the equality industry" and be the subject of state supported extortion.' He added that '80 per cent of the judgements are in favour of Travellers. The whole ethos of the equality industry is that the Travellers are right' (*Sunday Tribune* 7 July 2002). In fact, in 2002, 100 people, 96 of whom were Travellers, brought their cases of discrimination by licensed premises to the Equality Tribunal and only 56 per cent of these cases were successful on the Traveller ground. On the same occasion Tadg O'Sullivan spoke of his refusal to deal with the Equality Authority in preparing a code of practice for licenced premises, stating 'if we cannot deal with state-funded organisations and state-funded terrorism on our own terms, then we have to say no thanks'. Hyperbole and inaccuracy emerge once again at the service of backlash.

Frank Fell was usually more measured but still declared that 'We see this thing as a total racket. It has turned itself into another industry and it is just a way of shutting down publicans' (*Sunday Tribune* 30 June 2002). He later pointed out that 'we don't think the claims are low. Up to December last the average per case was €2,920' (*Sunday Tribune* 7 July 2002). In fact, the Equality Tribunal figures for 2002 show that 59 people (56 of whom were Travellers) were successful in cases against licenced premises during the year with an average award in compensation of €930. No award at all was made in four of the successful cases. Frank Fell also suggested that in the case of many of the awards then being made the publicans might not have assessed the case properly and had not put forward a well thought-out defence. He added that individual publicans were no match for well-organised Travellers' organisations (*Sunday Tribune* 30 June 2002).

The vintners have influence. The Vintners Federation of

Ireland annual conference in 2002 passed a motion express-
ing concern at the manner in which the Equal Status Act
was being implemented. The motion condemned some of
the Equality Tribunal decisions and demanded action by
the Federation. The power of the vintners was highlighted in an *Irish Times* editorial which reflected on the debate
at this conference about both the Equal Status Act and the
proposed smoking ban: 'In normal circumstances the behaviour of the Vintners Federation of Ireland would be regarded as outrageous, but publicans have dictated their
own terms of behaviour to governments for such a long
time that their bullying approach is taken for granted. And
there is no reason to believe the new government, led by
Fianna Fáil, will respond in a different way to its predeces-
sors' (25 May 2002).

The vintners had a good year in 2002. The Equality
Authority, unfortunately, helped by making a mess of
a press release in January about a case taken against the
Glimmer Man pub in Dublin. The pub was found to have
discriminated against John Maughan, a visually impaired
Traveller,when it refused to serve him; it was late afternoon
and he was accompanied by his thirteen-year-old son and
his guide dog. The case was taken on the Traveller, disability and family status grounds. He won his case on the family
status ground because the pub had a 'no children' policy.

The Equality Tribunal found that having a blanket ban
on under eighteen-year-olds being in a pub with their parents was discriminatory against those parents on the family
status ground. The Tribunal clarified that this should not be
interpreted as meaning that in all circumstances publicans
must serve parents when accompanied by their children.
Our press release (6 January 2002) omitted the key word
'not'. Mayhem and confusion ensued. We put out a correc-
tion the next day after we spotted the error and I did a lot
of interviews to try and secure more accurate debate about

the case. This was to little effect.

The publicans went for the jugular. Tadg O'Sullivan said this 'was political correctness gone stark raving mad' and 'the idea that publicans will be able to do nothing about young children being on their premises at 1 am on a Saturday is daft' (*Irish Independent* 7 January 2002). Frank Fell weighed in with the comment that 'The people who made this decision must live in cloud cuckoo land' (*Irish Examiner* 7 January 2002). An editorial in the *Irish Examiner* stated that 'it will open us to the international ridicule of those who have traditionally caricatured our people as the drunken Irish. Can we blame them when they say only the Irish would make a law stipulating that drink must be served in the presence of children' (7 January 2002).

In the debate we also tried to highlight the importance of a family-friendly ethos within licensed premises. Such an ethos would promote a healthier drinking culture and a more inclusive social environment. Dan White was a lone supporting voice, writing in the *Evening Herald*: 'If Irish pubs are to have a future they must create an environment in which citizens of all ages can be made welcome and re-lax over a drink or a meal. In the meantime, families should take heart from the decision and refuse to be intimidated by these illegal bans' (8 January 2002).

Bryan Dobson of RTE's *Six One News* interviewed me in studio about the case and its fallout. In the chat beforehand I decided that he was not enthusiastic about the case and the interview was not going to be easy. Una O'Hagan was reading the news with Bryan Dobson that night. Just before the interview began, she told us about her experience of be-ing refused service when she had gone to a licensed prem-ises with her son after they had been out on a walk. This timely tale made an impression and contributed to a more open interview on the matter. But overall there was little support for the idea of a family-friendly pub.

John O'Donoghue, then Minister for Justice, Equality and Law Reform announced that the Government was going to amend the Equal Status Act to allow publicans to bar children from their premises at any time. He also announced that he was extending the terms of reference of the Commission on Liquor Licensing, which was due to report later that year, to examine the rights of publicans to refuse admission. This was bad news.

We went public to criticise this decision—a move that did not go down well with officials in the Department of Justice, Equality and Law Reform. However, we had to defend the equality legislation. The Minister's decision had set a dangerous precedent: misinformed public pressure and controversy had been sufficient to have the equality legislation amended. We criticised the composition of the Commission: it boded ill for the future when a Commission dominated by vintner, hotelier and restaurant interests with no representatives from equality organisations, was to consider matters of equality and non-discrimination in the admission practices of the publicans. Our inaccurate press release on the Glimmer Man case had opened the way for the vintners' organisations to progress their demand that publicans should have the right to refuse admission without having to give any reason.

The next development in 2002 on this issue was the move by the vintners to organise a blanket ban on serving Travellers. This was spearheaded by the Westport Vintners Association, then chaired by Chris Lavelle. He wanted to organise a blanket ban on Travellers by public houses in Westport. His activities were based on the favoured myth of backlash that equality had gone too far. This ban on Travellers would be in breach of the Equal Status Acts which make it a criminal offence to procure another person to engage in discrimination. He said 'I know we are breaking the law and I know we will be objected to. If that is going to happen it will happen. If we do not have control of our premises we are as well to close our doors' (www.breakingnews.ie 14 August 2002). By August 2002, media reports suggested that some two dozen pubs were involved in the ban in Westport (Independent.ie 8 August 2002). The Mayo Traveller Support Group organised a well-supported local petition to challenge the ban. The Vintners Federation of Ireland backed their colleagues in Westport and proposed to make the ban national. This would be il-legal under the Equal Status Act. Tadg O'Sullivan said he would go to jail rather than have 'VFI members and their families subjected to violence and terror by the travelling community' (Independent.ie 8 August 2002).

Willie O'Dea, then junior minister with responsibil-ity for equality, stepped into the breach. He did not ini-tially appear to be a promising candidate for mediator. In July, when he launched the Annual Report of the Equality Tribunal, he had stated that 'measures aimed at protecting vulnerable individuals or groups should not be misused by a small minority'. This appeared to indicate some sympa-thy with the vintners' thinking. However, he met with the vintners and with Traveller organisations and secured an end to the ban. The vintners promised to co-operate with the Equality Authority in compiling a code of practice on access to licensed premises. They did not co-operate. They were clearly still optimistic that the Commission on Liquor Licensing would solve their problems. The Traveller organ-isations agreed to make submissions to the Commission to assist their work on publicans' right to refuse and, despite reservations about the composition of the Commission, they did so.

Later that year the renewal of Chris Lavelle's licence was challenged by Bernadette Comiskey of the Mayo Traveller Support Group. Traveller groups expressed anger when his licence was renewed despite his disregard for the law in promoting a ban on serving all Travellers. Judge Mary Devins, who heard the licence renewal case, criticised the Vinters Federation for what she called a 'blatant, crude and calculated' attempt to have the Equal Status Act changed (Pavee Point *Newsletter* October 2002). The decision to re-new the licence was appealed to the Circuit Court. The mat-ter was settled, before the appeal was heard, on the basis of a promise from Chris Lavelle not to repeat the ban.

The final and defining development during 2002 was, in effect, the cave-in to the vintners' pressure when the Commission on Liquor Licensing reported in December that year. The Equality Authority had had a tense relation-ship with the Commission having criticised its composition as inappropriate to review publicans' right to refuse admis-sion. We wrote to seek a meeting with chairperson Gordon Holmes but he felt unable to grant this request. There the matter rested. Gordon Holmes then seized the initiative and accused us of boycotting the Commission. He said 'We got boycotted by the Equality Authority. Bearing in mind that the Government directed us to deal with this issue and bearing in mind that the Equality Authority are totally Government funded, I find it surprising that they will not co-operate with a Government decision' (*Irish Examiner* 26 July 2002). He wasn't pulling any punches there—of course neither was he explaining why he had refused to meet us. After the resolution of the campaign to ban Travellers from pubs we decided, still with reservations, to make a sub-mission to the Commission despite the earlier refusal of its chairperson to meet with us. I met the subcommittee of the Commission working on this issue, along with Kate Hayes, then chairperson of the Equality Authority.

The Commission's report justified our fears. It recom-mended that licence holders should have discretion in re-lation to the presence of children on their premises and that restrictions on children in licensed premises should be retained. However, what was surprising was the inclusion of a full chapter on the equality infrastructure: this was not included in the terms of reference. One member of the Commission, who represented the Department of Education and Science, put in a reservation stating that the chapter should not be included. The Commission wrote that they did not 'wish to make any formal recommendations for legislative changes in relation to these matters since the primary focus in this report is on the liquor licensing code' but that it did wish 'to avail of this opportunity to put forward a number of suggestions arising from issues raised in the submissions' (*Report On Admission and Service in Licensed Premises*, Commission on Liquor Licensing, December 2002). The report went on to make damaging and unfair criticisms of the Equality Tribunal.

These criticisms reflected earlier statements by the vintners. Frank Fell had said 'There seems to be a lack of understanding by equality officers of the workings of the licensed trade. The Courts have a much broader view of life in general and a less ideological viewpoint' (*Sunday Tribune* 7 July 2002). Tadg O'Sullivan had said 'We have serious reservations about the sense of decisions by the [Equality Tribunal]' (*Sunday Independent* 12 May 2002).

The Commission report raised questions about the background and training of equality officers, suggesting that it was 'striking that a legal qualification is not considered necessary.' The report took issue with the structure of the Equality Tribunal and suggested it might be necessary to adjust this by 'the establishment of a panel selected by service providers and minority groups covered by the equality legislation' to hear cases. It raised concerns about the Tribunal's procedures and recommended that 'an independent study of procedural issues be undertaken to ensure fairness for complainants and respondents alike'. It was an extraordinary attack by a Commission with limited expertise in the area, without a mandate to examine this issue and which gave the Tribunal no right of reply. Most telling, however, was the statement in the report that 'The Commission advocates recourse to the District Court when dealing with all licensing issues.'

In May 2003, Michael McDowell, then Minister for Justice, Equality and Law Reform, announced that jurisdiction in dealing with allegations of discrimination by licensed premises would be transferred from the Equality Tribunal to the District Court. An editorial in the *Irish Examiner* suggested that the Minister 'should consider his position': 'Worrying signs of creeping authoritarianism, mixed with a growing disregard for the interests of minority groups, are manifest in the proposal by Justice Minister Michael McDowell to radically change the way this country's equality legislation operates' and 'Such a dramatic shift of legal responsibility after only three years experience of existing equality legislation, implies the Government is bowing to intense lobbying by vintners' (12 June 2003).

We took issue in the media with the decision of the Minister. We pointed out that the change of jurisdiction created new barriers for people seeking to take cases against licensed premises. Unlike the District Court, the Equality Tribunal has an investigative function, it offers mediation and does not award costs. The Tribunal offers a wider right of representation to the more legal setting of the District Court.

The change made by the Minister, therefore,was to a less accessible jurisdiction. Inevitably people stopped taking cases. Michael Clifford reported in the *Sunday Tribune* that only nine claims of discrimination were lodged in the District Court between September 2004 and February 2005 and compared this to an annual average of 516 claims received previously by the Equality Tribunal (19 June 2005). Backlash does work. The vintners were off the hook.

Department of Justice, Equality and Law Reform: a sacking

Early in May 2004, I was asked to meet an official of the Department of Justice, Equality and Law Reform in the Stephen's Green Hotel. I was given a letter stating that the official was directed by the Minister to advise me that my five-year contract terminated on 8 June 2004 and that this letter was to serve as notice of same. This was surprising, to put it mildly. At their meeting on 19 February the board of the Equality Authority had unanimously decided to re-appoint me on a permanent basis to the position of chief executive officer. The board was operating in conformity with the Employment Equality Acts. The Acts set out that the first chief executive officer was to be appointed by the Minister and that each subsequent chief executive officer, including any person re-appointed, was to be appointed by the board of the Equality Authority with the consent of the Minister. The Acts also state that this re-appointment could be done on such terms and conditions as the board decided, subject to the approval of the Minister and the consent of the Minister of Finance.

The official and I discussed the matter and I concluded by saying that I would be taking legal advice.

Four generous and skilled legal experts assisted me in fighting my sacking. They drafted and submitted a letter to the Department in response to the letter of notice I had received. This set out the board decision to re-appoint me and the legal basis on which it was made. It highlighted my reluctance to take legal proceedings if the matter was not resolved but notified the Department that I would do so if necessary. The board also decided to fight the matter. Their independence was being challenged by the Minister and their powers under the equality legislation were being undermined. They opened up ongoing contact with the

Department to resolve the matter.

In the middle of all this drama Minister Michael McDowell gave an interview to the *Irish Catholic*. In it he stated that 'a dynamic liberal economy like ours demands flexibility and inequality in some respects to function. It is this inequality which provides incentives' (27 May 2004). The interview caused quite a stir as it was a strange position for someone who was Minister with responsibility for equality. There were questions in the Dáil and national media coverage of his opinion. It also created the interesting possibility that the Minister with responsibility for equality, who felt that a bit of inequality was good for society, could shortly be in the High Court defending his decision to sack the chief executive officer of the Equality Authority in defiance of the Authority's board.

Tim Dalton, then secretary general of the Department of Justice, Equality and Law Reform, invited me to a meeting. He suggested a pause for reflection. I would be re-appointed for a short period to allow for further consideration on what was to be done. This did not seem advantageous given the situation that had been created by the Minister's interview. I declined.

The Department backed down. The Civil Service Act 1956 contains a provision that would allow my appointment to the position without a competition to fill the post if it was determined by Government that my appointment was 'in the public interest'. The Minister took this route. I was offered another five-year fixed term contract. The board of the Equality Authority was reluctant to accept this as the members felt it was in breach of the Protection of Employees (Fixed Term Work) Act 2003. They were of the opinion that this Act required I should now be put on a permanent basis having fulfilled one five-year fixed term contract.

The board managed this by deciding, at a meeting in

October 2004, to offer me the contract while formally clarifying that it was the board's view that there were no objective grounds justifying the renewal of my contract on a fixed term basis. This, in effect, brought me under the terms of the Protection of Employees (Fixed Term Work) Act and made me a permanent employee.

Department of Justice, Equality and Law Reform: decentralisation

The decentralisation issue began shortly before this incident but continued to dog the Equality authority for years afterwards.

Late in the afternoon of 3 December 2003 I got a call from Tim Dalton. Charlie McCreevy, Minister for Finance, was in the process of giving his budget speech in the Dail. Tim told me that the Minister had announced that 10,300 public servants were to be decentralised to 53 different locations around the country and that the Equality Authority was one of the bodies being decentralised. We were to be moved to Roscrea.

Decentralisation had been a focus for public debate since our establishment in 1999. That same year Charlie McCreevy had said that he wished to decentralise 10,000 public servants. He had been besieged by representations from all over the country seeking to benefit from this proposed programme. I was conscious at the time of the potential risk to the Equality Authority—loss of key expert staff, difficulty of access for clients, transitional risks etc. —and I and chairperson Kate Hayes met officials from the Department of Finance, and well-disposed Government ministers, to point out how destructive it would be for the new body to be included in any decentralisation programme.

In one meeting an official from the Department of Finance said that two lists had been prepared for the Minister, one of 6,000 posts they were recommending for decentralisation and another of 10,000 posts prepared on foot of the Minister's public promise. The Authority was on the longer list. The officials were not recommending this list to the Minister because they felt that the chaos attendant on this scale of decentralisation would destroy the public service.

The Minister had chosen to go with the second list. Decentralisation was, therefore, not just an attack on the Equality Authority, it was an attack on the whole of the public sector.

We commissioned Goodbody Economic Consultants to conduct a risk assessment of the proposed decentralisation to Roscrea. Goodbody reported that 'given the high and sustained level of risk that we have identified as associated with the proposed move of the Equality Authority to Roscrea, we consider that the Equality Authority cannot adequately perform its statutory functions from the new proposed location.'

It was clear that a location in Roscrea would pose significant barriers for people seeking to access the legal services of the Equality Authority. Goodbody Economic Consultants found that in 2003 47 per cent of calls to the Authority came from Dublin, 20 per cent from the rest of Leinster, 20 per cent from Munster and the remainder from Connaught and Ulster. People seeking the Authority's legal advice and representation—members of disadvantaged groups—would face barriers of limited public transport links, increased transport costs and possible overnight accommodation costs. Goodbody also pointed out that the Roscrea location would result in diminished direct access to the wide range of partner organisations working with the Authority. Necessary processes of persuasion, dialogue and negotiation could not be carried out at a distance.

Not one member of the staff said that he or she would move to Roscrea: 43 staff said they would not move and six staff said they did not know what they were going to do. Goodbody Economic Consultants found that two thirds of the staff saw their future career in the Equality Authority in Dublin, while none saw their future career with the Authority in Roscrea. Decentralisation would see the loss of all the expertise and experience built up in the Authority since its establishment in 1999.

We could not bring this analysis into the public domain since it was not possible to challenge what was now government policy. This made it somewhat difficult to mount a defence of the Authority. A number of non-governmental organisations did take a public stand on the issue. Gay HIV Strategies, the National Women's Council of Ireland, and Pavee Point Travellers Centre protested in the media and pointed to the barriers of accessibility that were being created. However, it proved difficult to sustain this protest.

Dan Murphy, general secretary of the Public Service Executive Union, stated that this decentralisation had 'more to do with getting a councillor elected in Roscrea than any plan to improve services to the public' (*The Irish Times* 5 December 2003). However, he also had to point out that the union was neither for nor against the idea of decentralisation as different staff had different needs.

In an interview in the *Irish Examiner*, Colm O Cinneide, a law lecturer based in London, pointed out that the British Equal Opportunities Commission 'visibly suffered when it was moved from London to Manchester'. He also suggested that the Equality Authority was included in the decentralisation programme because it was expendable. It was not important to Government. 'The Equality Authority in particular has an unrivalled international reputation and is regarded as a model of its kind. Moving its core operations to Roscrea could send the wrong message that it is somehow less important than other elements of Government' (11 December 2003).

The Roscrea Chamber of Commerce was, of course, delighted. The *Midland Tribune* reported a meeting where the Chamber congratulated Michael Smith, Minister for Defence, 'on the great news which will bring very positive and significant economic, social and cultural gains to Roscrea'. In turn, the Minister promised that work on the decentralisation of the Equality Authority would begin 'as early as January 2004' (13 December 2003). He was somewhat optimistic in this but it neatly illustrated Frank McDonald's analysis in *The Irish Times* that clientelist politics played a major role in the Government's decentralisation programme (4 December 2003).

In 2004, we were required to present a decentralisation implementation plan to the Department of Justice, Equality and Law Reform and to the Government's Decentralisation Implementation Group. This allowed us to put our concerns into the public domain as the plans were to be made public and were put up on the Department's website.

Chris Dooley of *The Irish Times* covered the implementation plans and noted that they 'expose a litany of problems which will be difficult and costly to overcome' (17 July 2004). He comes from Roscrea but happily managed to overcome any parochial bias, making particular reference to the problems facing the Equality Authority due to decentralisation including loss of skilled staff, exposure to risk of court action if casework went astray as a result of loss of staff, and additional costs. But as there was no sense of pressure behind the decentralisation programme over this period it was business as usual at the Equality Authority, despite staff morale taking a hit.

The appointment of Seán Aylward as secretary general of the Department of Justice, Equality and Law Reform changed this. He set out to fast track decentralisation in the justice sector. In July 2005 I was called to a meeting with him, his assistant secretary Noel Waters and their decentralisation official Martin McDonald. This was not a friendly encounter. I was told that the Equality Authority was the most uncooperative organisation in the justice sector, and I was the most uncooperative chief executive officer. I protested. The only concrete evidence put forward for this assertion was the risk assessment report we had commissioned from Goodbody Economic Consultants. I was told I now needed to sign off on a site in Roscrea and that staff from other Departments who wished to move to Roscrea would be rotated into the Equality Authority.

However, even at this point little progress was made. I went to Roscrea with Karen Erwin, then chairperson of the Authority, to tour four clearly unsuitable sites identified by the Office of Public Works. We chose one site but it eventually fell through, though we never heard why. Staff rotation did not occur because the only people who wanted to go to Roscrea were already there and were not available to be rotated into an office based in Dublin.

The prospect of elections in 2007 changed the situation. The Authority was instructed by the Department of Justice, Equality and Law Reform to move an advance party of 20 people to Roscrea by early 2007. The Department had secured temporary premises in Birchgrove House, a stately home converted into offices, that lies a few kilometres outside Roscrea. The board of the Authority pointed out that it would be impossibile to establish such an advance party, citing the unsuitability of temporary premises that were inaccessible to people with disabilities and the damage it would do to the organisation to lose such a large number of its staff in such a short space of time, given that no existing staff members would move to Roscrea. A tense stand-off ensued.

This was resolved on the basis of a deal with Seán Aylward. The Equality Authority would set up an advance office with 15 staff moving to Roscrea. The Authority would be allowed to retain 15 staff in its Dublin office in Clonmel Street after decentralisation. The costs of the advance party would also be fully met by the Department. There was an additional gain in this for the Equality Authority. At the time we had seven staff vacancies which had not been filled for some years—an all too common situation in the civil service. These were the first seven posts decentralised to Roscrea which meant that we had our full staffing complement for the first time since our establishment in 1999.

Michael McDowell opened the advance office in May 2007. This was just before the elections and Minister of State Tom Parlon also attended. Ironically, the opening could not take place in Birchgrove House because it was inaccessible to people with disabilities. It was felt that this contradiction might be used to embarrass the Minister. The opening therefore actually took place in the historic Black Mills Centre in the middle of Roscrea.

Department of Justice, Equality and Law Reform: in the Supreme Court

In January 2006 we applied for the right to appear as *amicus curiae* (friend of the Court) in a case before the High Court. The case was being taken by a Traveller family, with the help of the Irish Traveller Movement. It was being taken against two local housing authorities, the Commissioner of An Garda Síochána, the Director of Public Prosecutions, the District Justice sitting in Ballina, Ireland and the Attorney General. The Traveller family sought to challenge the failure of the relevant housing authorities to meet their accommodation needs. They also sought to challenge the Criminal Justice (Public Order) Act which had introduced new provisions in relation to trespass on the basis that it had a disproportionate and discriminatory impact on Travellers. The organisations against whom the case was taken did not oppose our application to be joined to the case as *amicus curiae.*

The judge gave us liberty to appear as *amicus curiae* to assist the Court with our specialist knowledge of national and European equality legislation and in particular in relation to the application and interpretation of the EU 'Race' Directive should it arise as part of the case. Unlike the Irish Human Rights Commission, the enabling Acts do not give the Equality Authority explicit power to appear as *amicus curiae* in cases, so the judge's decision set an important precedent.

In March 2006 we again sought leave to appear as *amicus curiae*, on the invitation of the plaintiffs' representatives, in a case before the High Court. This case was taken by two older Travellers, supported by the Irish Traveller Movement. They were in poor health and were seeking habitable accommodation from their local housing authority through the provision of a caravan. The case was taken against South Dublin County Council, the Minister for the Environment, Heritage and Local Government, Ireland and the Attorney General. They all opposed our application to act as *amicus curiae*. It was made clear to us that this was at the instigation of the Department of Justice, Equality and Law Reform. This was going to delay matters for the Traveller couple.

In May 2006, the High Court judge ruled in our favour. He said that we had a *bona fide* interest in the matter, and that where there was no statutory provision for us to act as *amicus curiae*, the Court had jurisdiction in the matter where it might be of assistance to the Court. He also said that it was incidental to the powers of the Equality Authority to assist the Court as *amicus curiae*. In a surprise move this decision was then appealed to the Supreme Court.

At the end of October 2006, in a majority judgement delivered by Mr Justice Fennelly, the Supreme Court dismissed the appeal. Mr Justice Fennelly stated that 'the

Authority has the statutory authority to apply to act and, if permitted by the court, to act as *amicus curiae*. In my opinion, that power falls well within the scope of the general power of the Authority. It is not merely ancillary or incidental. It is, however, a power of comparatively modest proportions compared with the broad and general powers of the Authority. It is a power to intervene in court proceedings in circumstances where the Authority considers it can assist the court in reaching a conclusion.'

The Department of Justice, Equality and Law Reform, in seeking to ensure that we did not go too far, had instigated a legal process that went as far as the highest court in the land, incurring significant expense and delaying the case of the Traveller couple who were in serious need due to ill health, and all in vain.

But now things took an even more difficult turn. Although government and public sector officials remained at ease with according people the right not to be discriminated against, they became increasingly averse to those rights actually being exercised—and in particular by individuals against the public sector. The Equality Authority had become a target because it provided legal advice and representation to these people. The limited commitment to fairness that underpins equality of opportunity was, in my opinion, now to be contested. A coup, to use the words of Senator Ivana Bacik, was in the offing.

5. 'A quiet coup'

The process of bringing the Equality Authority to heel accelerated in August 2007 when our new board was due to be announced. I was on holiday at the time but got a call from an official in the Department of Justice, Equality and Law Reform giving me the names. Alarm bells rang—not a single member from the previous board had been reappointed. Holiday spirits were somewhat dampened as I feared that I would probably be the next to go.

The new board, formally appointed in September, did not look promising as it lacked any institutional memory of the Authority's work and development. Angela Kerins, the new chairperson, was known to be close to Fianna Fáil and to be a friend of Seán Aylward, secretary general of the Department of Justice, Equality and Law Reform. She and two other members were on the board of the National Disability Authority which she also chaired; another board member represented a disability organisation. This seemed a disproportionate voice in a board of only twelve members for what is just one of the nine grounds covered by the equality legislation. Angela Kerins was also a member of the National Executive Council of IBEC, which, as was custom, had two nominees on the new board.

It appeared, at first, that the new chairperson might have a clear run within this board. However, things did not unfold as might have been expected: new board members emerged as having ideas of their own and the process of bringing the Authority to heel got bogged down in struggles at board level.

Early issues

Two points of attack emerged. First, Angela Kerins stated that she wished to be the primary media spokesperson for the Equality Authority. This had always been my responsibility. Second, my role in the process for selecting cases to be supported was questioned. The board commissioned an external consulting company, HELM, to conduct a review of corporate governance and set up a corporate governance review committee. The previous board had put in place a very detailed code of governance. This set out my role as chief executive officer and established that I was the primary spokesperson for the Equality Authority, and that I selected the cases to be progressed on the basis of criteria set down by the board. A legal committee of the board monitored my decisions. These were the first shots in what was, in my view, to emerge as a coup at the Equality Authority.

The HELM review stated: 'Given the high profile of the organisation and the current complexity and range of the communications brief, and the fact that the Board consists of new appointees, communication becomes a prime consideration in relation to governance.' It went on to recommend: 'The Chairperson, as titular head of the Authority, should assume the role of primary spokesperson for communication.'

It is not clear how HELM came to this conclusion. The recommendation did not sit easily with another conclusion in their report that 'the executive and non-executive responsibilities are clear and function well in supporting governance' in the Authority.

Resistance to the coup now emerged within the board. The corporate governance review committee met in February 2008 to consider the HELM report. The committee split down the middle on the recommendation concerning the primary spokesperson for communications for the organisation. A decision to change the existing code of governance could not therefore be brought to the board. Instead it was decided that Angela Kerins and I were to come up with a proposal to resolve the issue.

Angela Kerins then requested clarification from the Department of Justice, Equality and Law Reform as to the role of the chairperson. The secretary general, Seán Aylward, replied that 'The Chairperson has particular responsibility for providing strategic leadership on matters such as: formulating the Authority's strategy for discharging its statutory duties; encouraging high standards of propriety and promoting the efficient and effective use of staff and other resources throughout the organisation; and acting as Principal Spokesperson of the Authority.'

Tensions rose. Whispered conversations between board members in corridors before and after board meetings sought to advance the issue. No further meetings of the corporate governance review committee were convened until after four more board members were appointed in July 2008. The equality legislation had to be amended by the Oireachtas to enable these additional appointments. The new members included an official of the Department of Justice, Equality and Law Reform and another member of the board of the National Disability Authority, Christy Lynch, who was immediately appointed vice chairperson. These two new members were appointed to the corporate governance review committee. However, despite the additional members, when the committee subsequently reconvened to consider a new code of governance drafted by HELM, it again split down the middle on the question of who should be the primary spokesperson. The committee decided to refer the issue to the full board. It was never resolved and I remained as primary spokesperson.

The question of my role in the selection of cases to support was first raised in a phone call from Angela Kerins in

April 2008. She told me that the chairperson of the legal committee, which monitored my decisions, had raised the matter with her. She intended to obtain independent legal advice on issues such as delays that might arise if my selection role was rescinded. I protested against this further proposed diminution of my role and the bypassing of the Equality Authority's own legal advisor in seeking legal advice externally.

A legal committee meeting was held later that month. A member of this committee proposed a motion that the committee was pleased with the delegation of case selection to me and with the manner in which this delegation was being exercised. All but the chairperson agreed with this motion. The board eventually confirmed my role and I continued to select the cases for support.

Board resistance had won the day. This phase of the coup was unsuccessful. The voice and profile of the Equality Authority was sustained and the legal strategy was safeguarded. Nearly a year had passed and, despite reinforcements, the coup was stalled. This was a tribute to the integrity, expertise and commitment of a number of board members who held to their principled position on the importance of an effective and independent Equality Authority. It was a temporary reprieve.

Merger proposal

On 24 July 2008, a report appeared in *The Irish Times* of a meeting between the heads of the agencies in the justice and equality sector and Seán Aylward. I had attended that meeting. Deaglán De Bréadún wrote that the Government was proposing to merge the Equality Authority, the Irish Human Rights Commission and the Office of the Data Protection Commissioner into a single agency. The leak turned what had been only a proposal from the Department of Finance into something more akin to a fait accompli.

There were actually five agencies involved in the proposal — the Equality Tribunal and the National Disability Authority were also on the list. It was strange that only three of these organisations had been mentioned in the leak to the media: was the leak a signal of actual official thinking?

More than forty agencies come under the Department of Justice, Equality and Law Reform. No reason was given for the focus on these five agencies nor was any rationale given by the Department of Finance for the proposed amalgamation. The letter from the Department of Finance to the Department of Justice containing the merger proposal merely stated that the aim of the proposals, which were being made to all departments, was to save €20 million in 2009. This was just before the looming global financial crisis hit the headlines, and the parlous state of Ireland's public finances became clear. The Department of Finance stated that details of the proposals could be altered but not the total sum to be saved.

At the meeting, Seán Aylward said that the Government was concerned to simplify the service delivery landscape; he also said that the Government wished to assert its authority. He said that arguments as to whether or not savings would be achieved would have no impact on the final decision. The five agencies were given until 15 September 2008 to respond to the proposal.

Mary Robinson, former President of Ireland, defended the Equality Authority and the Irish Human Rights Commission at a conference in August to mark the 40th anniversary of the North's civil rights movement. She said: 'There should be no erosion of the powers of these bodies. They should never be reduced by merging or in any other way.' Agencies like the Equality Authority 'need to be invigorated, not pared down on the cheap'. She added a key point that 'human rights belong to the people and are to hold those in power to account' (*Irish Times* 25 Aug. 2008).

Joe Costelloe of the Labour Party opened up political opposition to the merger when he said: 'It now seems that the tightened Exchequer situation is going to be used to neuter organisations like the Human Rights Commission and the Equality Authority that have been critical of the Government' (*The Irish Times* 20 August 2008).

Senator Ivana Bacik identified a 'quiet coup' taking place as 'with the Dáil and Seanad on vacation, a recession looming and everybody desperately seeking sunshine abroad, the Government has been discreetly making plans to neuter a number of agencies carrying out vital functions in upholding human rights standards' (*Irish Independent* 15 September 2008). She called for 'loud political and legal resistance'.

Charlie Flanagan of Fine Gael also entered the fray. He said that 'Fianna Fáil was making a mess of reforming state agencies by proposing to abolish ones that did a good job while leaving ineffective ones untouched' (*Sunday Times* 21 September 2008).

Joanna McMinn, then director of the National Women's Council of Ireland, led resistance from the community and voluntary sector. She began to convene meetings of a broad range of civil society groups to develop and pursue a campaign to stop the merger. The groups, which included OPEN, Pavee Point, Congress, SIPTU, the Carers' Association, the Irish Traveller Movement, Inclusion Ireland, GLEN, the Migrant Rights Centre of Ireland, Amnesty and the Irish Council of Civil Liberties eventually formed what is now called the Equality and Rights Alliance.

The board of the Equality Authority made its position known on 11 September 2008. It was opposed to the merger and set out three reasons for its opposition.

1) The merger would diminish the capacity of the Equality Authority to provide information, legal advice and legal representation to those who experience discrimination as

well as its capacity to provide advice to employers and service providers on good practice in promoting equality. There was a strong case for maintaining this specific institutional focus on equality, diversity and discrimination at a time when there was evidence of significant unmet need across all sectors for the supports provided by the Equality Authority.

2) The five agencies to be merged had a wide range of different and even incompatible functions. Constitutional issues of fair procedure and natural justice could arise where the Equality Authority and the Equality Tribunal formed part of the same body. It would be inappropriate to merge the Office of the Data Protection Commissioner with four bodies that it currently regulated in relation to the data they held. Further incompatibilities would arise where an advisory body (National Disability Authority), a body defending human rights (Irish Human Rights Commission) and a body promoting equality with a mandate to contribute to social change (Equality Authority) would have different working methods and approaches to working with employers, service providers, policy makers and individuals experiencing discrimination or abuse of their human rights.

3) There would be significant costs in establishing the new organisation with only small financial savings and no operational benefit to the five agencies. They were small, low budget organisations and there was no overlap of functions between them. Any cost/benefit analysis would say no to this proposal.

In the press release issued by the Equality Authority, Angela Kerins stated that 'the Equality Authority is, in its current form, both effective and efficient in carrying out its mandate and it should be retained as it is. The merger proposal will only serve to disadvantage those who are already disadvantaged in our society.' The Equality Authority also suggested that, in line with the recent OECD review of the public sector, it would be happy to explore a better networking between agencies and the use of shared services as a means of securing savings.

Budget cut

Budget day, 14 October 2008, was the day the merger proposal was to be announced. I was given no advance warning of what had been decided. During the afternoon, staff members were glued to the Internet and to the radio. The first news was good. There was no talk of mergers or amalgamations. Relief and even celebration spread throughout the building. It was announced that we were to integrate our facilities, back offices, administrative services and access for citizens with the Irish Human Rights Commission. There was nothing too damaging in that requirement. It appeared that the Department of Justice, Equality and Law Reform proposal had got shot down at Cabinet and this latest phase in the coup had failed. Later that afternoon, celebration turned to dismay when some of our staff found further details of the budget on the Internet. The Equality Authority was in real trouble. First up was decentralisation. It was announced that all organisations which did not yet have a permanent premises in their decentralised location could defer decentralisation until 2011. The Authority was an exception: a further 15 staff were to be moved to our temporary premises in Roscrea. Worse was to come. We discovered that our budget was to be cut by 43 per cent, from €5.897 million to €3.333 million. This was way beyond any cut made to any other organisation in the justice and equality sector. The National Disability Authority, for example, was cut by 2 per cent, the Office of the Data Protection Commissioner by 9 per cent and the Equality Tribunal had an increase of 15 per cent. Only the Irish Human Rights Commission had a comparable cut—24 per cent.

The political exchanges in the Dáil on the Equality Authority were sharp. In a debate on 13 November 2008 Pat Rabbitte of the Labour Party asked 'Why has the Minister decided to kill the Equality Authority?' He went on: 'The Equality Authority is being singled out in a vindictive manner because officials in the Department of Justice, Equality and Law Reform do not like what it has been doing.' Charlie Flanagan of Fine Gael said that 'As a result of these cutbacks . . . the Equality Authority will have very little ability to pursue its core objectives.' He added: 'This is a hatchet job.' (*Parliamentary Debates (Official Report — Unrevised*) Dáil Éireann Thursday 13 November 2008).

Tensions arose between the Green Party and Fianna Fáil. Ciaran Cuffe from the Green Party told the Oireachtas Committee on Justice, Defence, Equality and Women's Rights that he was opposed to Government policy on cutting the budgets of human rights bodies. He said that these cutbacks went 'far beyond fiscal savings'. He said that he had brought his arguments to his colleagues in Government and he hoped there would be some room for manoeuvre (*The Irish Times* 11 December 2008).

Civil society also sought to defend the Equality Authority and the Irish Human Rights Commission. The Equality and Rights Alliance grew in strength and numbers and constantly challenged what was happening to the Equality Authority. It held public meetings, put out press releases, had Dáil questions put down and made representations to Dáil committees. The Alliance asserted at every opportunity that the cover of the deepening recession was being used to neutralise what Deagán De Bréadún had described as 'a thorn in the side of the establishment . . . due to its meticulous pursuit of its remit' (*The Irish Times* 24 July 2008) but it was difficult to get the message across that what was happening to the Equality Authority had nothing to do with managing the public finances.

Media commentary was limited. Recession, a hugely un-popular budget and the banking crisis dominated the news. Carol Coulter of *The Irish Times* was the exception. She wrote that decentralisation and budget cutbacks 'inevitably call into question the ability of the Equality Authority to fulfill its mandate under the legislation that set it up'. She pointed out that 'the amount of money saved will be miniscule in the overall budget of the Department of Justice'. She noted that the 'majority of cases are taken by individuals who are claiming discrimination by the state and its agencies' and that 'it is hard to avoid the conclusion that this activity on the part of the Equality Authority has been an irritant to civil servants, and the opportunity afforded by the Budget to cut it short proved too hard to resist.' She went on to suggest that 'other bodies which scrutinise the workings of agencies of the state will have reason to be worried', making specific mention of the Garda Ombudsman Commission and the Office of the Ombudsman (11 November 2008).

The Equality Authority board met on 10 November, nearly one month after the announcement, to consider a briefing paper I had prepared on the impact of the budget. Due to the cutback current casework commitments could not be met and the capacity to open new case files would be severely curtailed. The Authority would not be able to as-sist clients whose cases were appealed to the higher courts. Inquiries now being considered for implementation by the Authority could not progress. Targeted public information campaigns which played a valuable role in raising aware-ness of the equality legislation would no longer be possi-ble. Research work would be significantly reduced. Work to support good practice by employers and service provid-ers would be compromised because although the Authority had secured EU funds for this work it would not have the matching funds required.

The board agreed a plan to manage this situation and

sought a meeting with Dermot Ahern, the Minister for Justice, Equality and Law Reform. It put out a press statement stating that the proposed decentralisation and the budget cutback 'if fully implemented, may render the Equality Authority unable to fully or effectively carry out the full range of its core functions under the equality legislation and relevant EU Directives'. It went on to stress that the functions of the Equality Authority to promote equality and combat discrimination were 'particularly important at a time of economic downturn for people experiencing inequality, as it is these groups who are most vulnerable in such a period'. Nearly a month later, on 10 December, Dermot Ahern finally met the Authority.

This meeting was the final tipping point in the coup. There was a bizarre opening exchange prior to the meeting itself. The Authority wanted the full board to attend. However, it was told that the Minister's 'diary is very full at the moment and he has quite a short window of time for the meeting'. He requested that the meeting be confined to Angela Kerins and myself. The board then sought to have five or six members present at the meeting. The reply came back that 'the room is very small, as is the table'. They could not accommodate the large delegation but they would allow Christy Lynch, the vice chairperson, to attend.

The room was full. We went in to meet the Minister to find him encircled by five of his senior officials. None of them had anything much to contribute during the meeting. It seemed that these five men in their dark suits were just there as witnesses to the final act in the rather long drawn out coup that had been prosecuted against the Equality Authority.

The board had agreed a management plan to deal with the budget cutback without compromising our functions. This sought to retain all the staff and to develop more labour intensive approaches to fulfilling our functions so as to achieve the required savings in our non pay budget. The plan involved prioritising initiatives that could avail of EU funding in supporting good practice by employers and service providers. It limited legal work to supporting casework at a minimal level, rather than conducting inquiries, so as to maintain a culture of compliance with the equality legislation. This plan, which was not over ambitious, involved a significant decrease in activity and still meant operating a budget cutback of 32 per cent. We asked for €700,000, to enable implementation of this plan, to be added to the diminished budget of €3.333 million.

I presented the plan to the Minister. He said he could not accept it and that he made no apologies for prioritising the fight against crime. He was not able to provide the additional €700,000 requested.

Angela Kerins responded to the Minister saying, in effect, that this was a pity but that he could count on us to do our best. I pointed out to the Minister that we might not be able to carry out all our functions with the reduced budget and that the cut ran counter to a commitment he had made that agencies under his remit would retain funding for their core activities. Angela Kerins intervened to tell the Minister that we could carry out our functions and that we would.

I asked why the Equality Authority was subject to such a disproportionate cut in its budget compared to other agencies in the Department. Neither the Minister nor the assembled leadership of the Department could explain this decision. I pointed out the damage to the capacity of the Equality Authority that would result from further decentralisation and queried why it was continuing for us when it was on hold until 2011 for all other agencies. No explanation was given.

The Minister went on to say that he could not guarantee that the budgetary situation for the Equality Authority would not get worse over the coming year and indeed that the merger proposal with the Irish Human Rights Commission was still under consideration.

That pretty much was that. As I left the meeting I could hear Christy Lynch mending fences by apologising to Seán Aylward for troubling them with this meeting, saying that it had been unavoidable.

Then it was down to the Dáil bar for tea, coffee and reviewing. Angela Kerins and Christy Lynch were clear. The challenge now was to set out and implement a strategy to get the Department 'to love us'. The second priority was to start preparing for a merger so that we could outmanoeuvre what were deemed to be the expansionist ambitions of the Irish Human Rights Commission.

The meeting with the Minister had made it clear to me that we had lost any hope of carrying out our work effectively. The reviewing in the Dáil bar showed me that our independence was also a casualty of the coup. I knew that I could not continue as chief executive officer in these circumstances.

Resignation

I had already decided, before the meeting with the Minister, that I would resign if the management plan was not accepted. I was not surprised at the outcome and yet I still found it hard to believe that the Minister would reject the plan. The battle within the Equality Authority was over. I felt a desperate sense of loss in that defeat.

I resigned the next day, 11 December. My resignation merely moved the site of battle outside the Authority. There was a sense of unreality to it for me. It was like a bad dream being played out. My real feelings were essentially parked until there was time for reflection after the full battle had played itself out.

The most difficult part of resigning was telling the staff.

At a meeting on 11 December I explained that in my view the Equality Authority had been rendered unviable. I could not lead and implement the necessary dismantling of an organisation that we had all worked together to build up over the previous ten years. I was not willing to pretend that the Equality Authority was anything other than unviable from this point on, a pretence that would have been required of me. I felt bound to expose exactly what was happening to the Equality Authority and why it was happening but this would not be possible if I remained as chief executive officer. I could not offer any optimism as the outlook was bleak for the organisation and for the staff's future in the organisation. It was a very sad occasion for us all and I left the room upset and disorientated.

The news of my resignation broke in the media on 12 December. For the first time for a long time I was able to present a clear message. I said that the work of the Equality Authority was fatally compromised by the strategy of the Department of Justice, Equality and Law Reform in the budget. I stated my view that Minister Dermot Ahern's rationale for the 43 per cent cutback, that he sought to prioritise the fight against crime, was simply not credible. I pointed out that the only credible explanation was that the Authority's casework strategy, particularly in relation to allegations of discrimination in the public sector, had been experienced as a threat by senior civil servants and/ or Government. I suggested that the Equality Authority was being silenced for being an awkward witness to the inequality and discrimination in our society.

Angela Kerins was quick to issue a press release paying tribute to me. She said that the work of the Equality Authority was recognised by the Minister and that he regretted having to impose the cuts. It was strange that the chairperson of the Equality Authority should be speaking on behalf of the Minister. In contrast to the statement issued by the board in November on the budget cutback, she went on to say that 'While I accept that the reduction in the Authority's budget will have an impact on our work, I am confident that we will be able to carry out our core functions, but in a more limited and prioritised way' (*Irish Independent* 12 December 2008).

The Minister and the Department were silent. However, unidentified Department spokespeople kept spinning away to the media. They sought to trivialise my position by suggesting that my concerns over decentralisation were due to a bat infestation in the Authority's advance premises in Roscrea. The *Star* quoted a spokesperson as saying that 'A family of bats were removed after being cited by Mr Crowley as a reason why they couldn't decentralise' (*Star* 13 December 2008). I had raised the question of the bats some months previously as they were creating unpleasant conditions for the staff already in Roscrea. But this was no big issue and had already resolved itself as the bats left for more favourable climes long before I resigned.

The *Sunday Times* headlined its coverage 'When equality took a back seat to empire building'. They suggested that the 'Equality Authority became engorged during the boom years, its voracious appetite for public cash appearing to grow with feeding' (14 December 2008). They used figures presented to the Dáil by Dermot Ahern to state that our annual budget had grown from €378,000 in the year of our establishment to a current €5.9 million. What was left unsaid in the Dáil was that the Equality Authority was established in October of 1999 and thus the figure of €378,000 covered only a short set-up period. The real comparison should have been with the annual budget of €3.787 million for the year 2001, the Equality Authority's first fully operational year following the enactment of the Employment Equality Acts and the Equal Status Acts.

The *Mail On Sunday* 'learned' that the Minister had

turned down a request for €110,000 to mount the Supreme Court appeal against Portmarnock Golf Club's male-only policy and suggested that it was this refusal, rather than any principled stance, that lay behind my resignation (28 December 2008). There had been no discussion of this at the meeting with the Minister. We had included the risk of the costs of the Pormarnock case as one example in a list of payments that could be covered by the Department if it wished to secure our viability by taking on some of our costs rather than by giving us additional funding. This was a payment that would only be required if the case was lost. The list was never discussed, as the possibility of anything at all being paid for by the Department was immediately rejected at the meeting with the Minister.

Kevin Myers, now with the *Irish Independent*, welcomed my resignation. I think it was probably the first time he got the name of the organisation right. The resignation, he wrote, was 'easily the greatest contribution he could have made to this state' adding that 'The Equality Authority was one of the most grisly and ruinous public bodies in a decade of grisly and ruinous state-driven political correctness' (19 December 2008).

John Waters also welcomed the changes to the Equality Authority. He wrote in *The Irish Times* that 'Far from being the end of the equalisation of Irish society, then, the departure of Niall Crowley and the board members who support him may offer, for the first time, an opportunity to promote a true concept of equality in Irish society' (6 February 2009). His big problem, as a proponent of men's rights, was that I was 'notoriously reticent about helping men to combat the truly grotesque forms of discrimination' they face.

But there was support too. In January 2009, in an important act of solidarity, all seven Saoithe of Aosdána signed a letter to *The Irish Times* to 'express our grave concern at the position of the Equality Authority'. The Saoithe, Seoirse

Bodley, Anthony Cronin, Brian Friel, Séamus Heaney, Louis Le Brocquy, Patrick Scott, and Camille Souter wrote 'there will be serious adverse consequences for people experiencing discrimination' and requested the Department 'to restore as a matter of urgency adequate funding to the Equality Authority'. This was an extaordinary and unprecedented intervention on the part of seven artists who have been recognised by their peers for their outstanding achievements.

By January 2009, six members of the board had resigned in protest at the cutbacks: Dennis O'Flynn, from Irish Distillers, and Finola McDonnell from IBEC, both IBEC nominees; Louise O'Donnell, from Impact, and David Joyce from Congress, both Congress nominees; Frank Goodwin of the Carers' Association and Therese Murphy of the National Women's Council of Ireland. They had been at the heart of the battle at board level since August 2007 to maintain an effective and independent Equality Authority. The resignation of the nominees of the social partners Congress and IBEC was unprecedented.

David Joyce said that the Equality Authority was becoming 'a pale imitation of the strong independent advocate for equality that the Authority has been since its inception' (*The Irish Times* 20 January 2009). Frank Goodwin said that the board was being forced to reconfigure its plans in a way that he considered compromised its independence. Therese Murphy said that the cuts 'have rendered the authority unable to do the job it was established to do' (*Irish Independent* 17 December 2008).

In her resignation statement, Louise O'Donnell expressed 'great concern' at the direction in which Angela Kerins was taking the organisation as 'she has clearly indicated that she wishes to diminish the role of professional people within the organisation and to move the organisation away from its role as advocate for those who cannot represent themselves' (*The Irish Times* 20 January 2009).

There were political battles in the Dáil and Seanad on the Equality Authority. The Dáil was briefly suspended during one debate. Pat Rabbitte of the Labour Party pressed Minister Dermot Ahern on Seán Aylward's role in the decision to cut the funding to the Equality Authority by 43 per cent. Bitter exchanges followed with Pat Rabbitte calling the Minister 'a petty little man'. The Minister at one point refused to resume his seat at the request of the Leas Cheann Comhairle and also declared that Pat Rabbitte was 'a disgrace, trying to denigrate a good public servant' (*Parliamentary Debates (Official Report — Unrevised*) Dáil Eireann 19 December 2008).

Green Party senators Dan Boyle and Deirdre de Burca purposely absented themselves from the Senate chamber when a vote was taken on an amendment put down by Senator David Norris condemning the Government's treatment of the Equality Authority. David Norris questioned the actions of Angela Kerins in relation to the press statement issued after my resignation saying 'I have never seen such an extraordinary act of treachery' (*The Irish Times* 17 December 2008). Dan Boyle was reported as saying that he had expressed his unhappiness over the funding reduction decision and that he believed that there were unelected influences within the area of government that were having a disproportionate effect and that there were personal agendas and biases that were informing policy in this area (*The Irish Times* 17 December 2008).

In the meantime, the Green Party had been seeking to negotiate a new deal for the Authority. In his opening address at its national convention in March 2009, John Gormley referred to the situation of the Equality Authority. He said that 'At our membership meetings I undertook to have those changes reversed. And I'm very glad to report to you this evening that we have succeeded in our mission. The planned further decentralisation of staff has been stopped and a further review of funding for the Equality Authority undertaken to ensure that it can do its work effectively' (*The Irish Times* 7 March 2009).

The following month in the Dáil, Dermot Ahern rejected the suggestion that cuts to the budget of the Equality Authority would be reversed and stated that the number of staff in its Roscrea office would shortly increase from 15 to 23. The row between the parties continued behind the scenes. Later that month the Minister stated in the Dáil that he would review the Equality Authority's funding and pause its decentralisation. However, this was a very partial victory for the Green Party. Decentralisation was halted. But no changes were made to the funding arrangements and in July 2009 the Special Group on Public Service Numbers and Expenditure Programmes, chaired by Colm McCarthy, recommended a further cut of 10 per cent to the non-pay budget of the Equality Authority on top of the 43 per cent cut already imposed.

The coup was completed with the launch in March 2009 of a new strategic plan for the Equality Authority. Angela Kerins said that the Authority 'had a significant cutback in our budget. This may limit what we spend but not what we can achieve' (*Irish Examiner* 5 March 2009). John Waters marked the change in direction with his first ever favourable opinion piece on the Equality Authority. He attended the launch of the plan and wrote that 'for the first time in many years I felt at home in a place where hitherto I would have found large tracts of carpet opening up around me'(*The Irish Times* 6 March 2009).

The factors behind the coup

Clearly, the apparent official commitment to equality has been thoroughly undermined, and the Equality Authority was one of the casualties of this change in political will and administration commitment. There were three main factors at play that resulted in even the limited ambition of fairness enshrined in the legislation losing support and the Authority becoming a particular target for attack.

Firstly, at a political level the enthusiasm for equality waned. This was partly because of the influence of the Progressive Democrats, and in particular, Michael McDowell, Minister for Justice, Equality and Law Reform from 2002 to 2007 , who was an articulate and forthright advocate of a more laissez-faire approach. Secondly, there was something counter-cultural about the work of the Equality Authority in Celtic Tiger Ireland. By championing those experiencing discrimination, it challenged the 'anything is possible, and everything is allowed' attitude. The Authority was an awkward witness to the inequality and discrimination in our wealthy society. The third and decisive factor was the resistance of the statutory sector which did not accept the Authority's independence and saw its activities as a threat.

There is a perspective in parts of government and of the statutory sector that suggests that people should be grateful for services provided. People have to be deserving, not demanding, of public support—it cannot be a matter of rights. But the equality legislation conferred limited rights of non-discrimination on people in receipt of public sector services. Supported by the Equality Authority, individuals exercised those rights to gain access to public sector services and to shape the way the services were provided.

In 2007, 69 per cent of Equality Authority case files under the Equal Status Acts related to allegations of discrimination by people availing of public sector services. Demands also came from public sector employees who sought to exercise their rights under the Employment Equality Acts: in 2007, 49 per cent of our case files under the Acts related to allegations of discrimination by employees of public sector bodies. It is my view that these allegations were experienced as a threat by Government and senior civil servants and this was a major reason for the budget cutback. It was these case files against the public sector that stimulated the coup at the Equality Authority.

The statutory sector is hierarchical. It is managed on an authoritarian basis and through the exercise of a top-down authority. The sector does not welcome advocacy from its employees, preferring obedience. Nor does the notion of an independent statutory equality body sit easily with this culture. It was clear that there was no understanding or acceptance of the independence required of the Equality Authority under the legislation and under the EU Equal Treatment Directives . This independence is essential if the Equality Authority is to be in any way effective in implementing its mandate. It was telling that Seán Aylward suggested that one reason for the proposed amalgamation of agencies was that government wished to assert its authority. The independence exercised by the Equality Authority contradicted this authoritarian culture and was one stimulus for the coup.

The coup revealed a determination in the Department of Justice, Equality and Law Reform which was not to be thwarted in this matter of bringing the Equality Authority into line. Each victory for those resisting the attack on the independence and effectiveness of the organisation was met with a new level of attack until success was achieved.

Hailed as a model of its kind throughout the EU, the Equality Authority was meticulous in implementing its mandate and careful not to stray beyond it. However, without political support the Equality Authority was vulnerable to attack.

We now have a situation where we have relatively progressive equality legislation but the institution to implement it has been rendered unviable. This is bad news for all who experience discrimination and, in particular, for those who take a case alleging discrimination. It is bad news for those leaders, advocates and catalysts who seek to use the equality legislation as a lever to achieve change in their places of work. It is bad news for Irish society as it fails to secure the real dividends to be had from a valuing of diversity and the achievement of equality.

The Equality and Rights Alliance has continued to challenge the budget cutbacks to the Equality Authority and to the Irish Human Rights Commission. The Alliance became more structured and secured funding to recruit staff. It submitted complaints to both the European Commission and the European Parliament that the budget cutback to the Equality Authority put Ireland in breach of the EU Equal Treatment Directives. These Directives require Ireland to have an organisation for the promotion of equal treatment with a capacity to provide 'independent assistance to victims of discrimination in pursuing their complaints about discrimination'. In my view, the cutback means there is no longer a statutory body with such a capacity in Ireland. However, in December 2009, the EU Commission decided not to launch infringement proceedings against Ireland on foot of the complaint. The Commission noted that it 'has always held the Equality Authority in Ireland in the greatest regard' and that it was 'with much regret that we learnt about the budget of the Equality Authority being reduced to the levels reported'. It stated that the European Directives 'are minimum-standards only and do not specify a particular level of funding or a particular organisational structure'. The lack of adequate detailed provisions in the EU Directives in relation to equality bodies left the European Commission with no ground to act on. The Commission was 'not convinced that the currrent level of budget is an an obstacle to the full performance of the tasks provided for by the Directives.' At the time of writing, the complaint to the European Parliament had yet to be heard.

It is valuable that the struggle for an independent and effective equality and human rights infrastructure is deemed by civil society to be a priority despite significant cutbacks in other key areas of the public sector. A response to the coup needs to go beyond seeking to oust those who have taken over or implementing some form of counter coup i.e. merely fixing the Equality Authority. The response needs to reflect on our slow and halting progress towards a more equal society in Ireland. A new political project is required with a real capacity to re-energise and advance our search for a more equal society.

The Equality and Rights Alliance has usefully begun to shift the debate. It has moved from seeking to repair a damaged institution to an acknowledgement that the statutory equality infrastructure that is now in place has deteriorated to a point that it is not reparable. It has set out to rethink both the institutions and the legislation that we have in place to promote equality and to combat discrimination. This may yet be the most important legacy from the coup at the Equality Authority—a new, more ambitious, and more effective infrastructure on which to build a more equal Ireland.

6. Towards a more equal society

After the coup

This coup at the Equality Authority marked a low point in the search for a more equal Ireland. It sent out a message that equality is not important. It set more limited boundaries to the ambition of those who advocate for greater equality in their organisations. It isolated and weakened those who would exercise their rights under equality legislation. It diminished the accountability of the state to those who experience inequality and discrimination.

In my view, the Equality Authority quickly became unviable during 2009. The scale of its work diminished and its staff complement was cut. The legal section was a particular focus for this downsizing, losing most of its experienced staff. The civil servants with expertise in casework were transferred back into the Department of Justice, Equality and Law Reform. Many of these legal staff had indicated a preference to stay working with the organisation. However, this was ignored.

The mantra of business as usual continued to be articulated by the Equality Authority. At the launch of the annual report for 2008 in September 2009, chairperson Angela Kerins stated: 'This annual report highlights the preparatory work undertaken by the Authority in planning for the continued effective delivery of the remit of the Authority into 2009 and beyond'. According to the report, the Equality Authority dealt with 10,443 queries in 2008 under the equality legislation and under legislation for statutory leave entitlements. This figure was queried in an investigative piece, by Michael Smith, in *Village Magazine*

(November-December 2009). I had presented a paper to the
board in November 2008 pointing out that by this date the
Authority had received only 7,737 queries. It was clear tha
Michael Smith knew this because this document had obvi-
usly been leaked to him. Using monthly averages for queries, Michael Smith questioned whether the annual report
was overstating the total number of queries dealt with by
1158 queries and went on to ask: 'Is diminished efficacy being masked?' The piece, which effectively captured the decline in the Equality Authority, concluded: 'It is clear that
the budgetary devastation and changes in personnel may
be sufficient to dispatch it to the political peripherality that
is the nemesis of the equality agenda.'

The Equality and Rights Alliance produced research in
November 2009 on the impact of the cuts on the Equality
Authority (*Downgrading Equality and Human Rights:
Assessing the Impact*, B. Harvey and Dr K. Walsh, Equality
and Rights Alliance, Dublin, 2009). The authors stated that
'The [promised] co-operation of the Equality Authority
in the research did not materialise in practice'. The report
identified a fall in legal queries to the Equality Authority
and a rapid closing of legal casework files it held. It pointed
to a decline in media coverage, fewer significant casework
outcomes, a much reduced engagement with the NGO
community and a sharp falling off of the equality agenda in
the business and enterprise community. The authors concluded: 'We question its [the Equality Authority's] ability
to carry out its mandate.' They also suggested that 'Any examination of the future of equality and human rights must
. . . include some consideration of alternative structures. It
is important to note that any new structures would require
both institutional and legislative reform.'

A new approach to equality

A more holistic and coherent approach to equality should

be a starting point when identifying an alternative structure. Policy and programmes in relation to equality in
Ireland have always been fragmented. Combating poverty
and seeking equality in access to resources, have been the
policy remit of the Department of Social and Family Affairs,
the statutory mandate of the Combat Poverty Agency and
the policy objective of the National Anti Poverty Strategy.
Promoting equality in a context of diversity and combating
discrimination have been the policy remit of the Department
of Justice, Equality and Law Reform, the statutory mandate
of the Equality Authority and the purpose of equality legislation. The only politician I ever heard suggesting a merger
of these related mandates was Mary Coughlan TD in 2003
when she was Minister for Social and Family Affairs. Even
then the proposal was made in jest.

The Equality Authority and the Combat Poverty Agency
had produced a report entitled *Poverty and Inequality* which
was launched in Dublin Castle by Minister Mary Coughlan.
The report was an attempt to ensure that anti-poverty policies and programmes addressed discrimination as a cause
of poverty and took account of the diversity of people living in poverty. I was sitting beside Helen Johnston, then
director of the Combat Poverty Agency, when the Minister
ad-libbed the first part of her speech. She addressed me
and Helen directly and told us we had made a very con-
vincing case for merging the Equality Authority and the
Combat Poverty Agency. We struggled unsuccessfully to
keep the looks of horror off our faces. The Minister took
visible pleasure in the spectacle before reassuring us that
she was not serious. In hindsight, I think we were wrong to
be so horrified.

The Combat Poverty Agency was established in 1986 to
advise the Minister for Social and Family Affairs on policy
to combat poverty, to implement projects to tackle poverty,
to examine the nature and causes of poverty and to build

a public understanding of poverty. It was subsumed into the Department of Social and Family Affairs in the October 2008 budget, the budget in which the Equality Authority's funding was cut by 43 per cent. Economic recession provided the cover for the Government to dismantle the two independent statutory organisations with a remit to progress equality through combating poverty and combating discrimination. The move coincided with a time of rising unemployment, increased poverty, high levels of discrimination and potential scapegoating of minorities. This does not bode well for people and groups experiencing inequality. It does not bode well for Irish society. However, the institutional vacuum that now exists does offer the possibility to imagine and pursue a new approach to promoting equality in a more integrated and effective manner.

Forms of injustice

Poverty and discrimination are two distinct forms of injustice but both create barriers to participation in society (*Redistribution or Recognition? A Political-philosophical Exchange*, Nancy Fraser and Axel Honneth, Verso, 2003). Poverty stops people from participating in society by limiting the means they have at their disposal. It is an economic phenomenon and reflects inequality in the distribution of the resources in society. Poverty is the result of inadequate redistribution in Irish society. Discrimination blocks people from participating in society by excluding them on the basis of their membership of a particular group. It is a cultural phenomenon in that it is based on people's identity and status. It reflects the unequal way institutions in society value diversity and different groups in society, and the lack of recognition and the low status and standing afforded to specific groups in society. However, while these are distinct forms of injustice, they are linked and are often experienced simultaneously.

Women, for example, experience both of these forms of injustice at the same time. They are more likely to be at risk of poverty than men. They earn less than men. Most part-time workers are women. Women spend substantially more time on unpaid caring and household work than men. Women thus experience significant and persistent economic inequalities. They are stereotyped as caring, dependent and passive. Domestic violence is predominantly experienced by women. Allegations of workplace discrimination on the gender ground are almost exclusively made by women under the Employment Equality Acts. Women thus experience significant and persistent cultural inequalities in being afforded lower status and standing than men.

These forms of injustice are interlinked. Economic inequality contributes to a context where women are afforded a lower status and standing than men due to their economic position. Discrimination and stereotyping contribute to this economic inequality by excluding women from economically advantageous positions and by shaping the choices made by, and the options open to, them.

Women also experience a further form of injustice that also blocks participation and which is a political phenomenon. This is evident in the absence of women from private sector boardrooms and from senior management positions in the public sector. It is evident in the low numbers of women in the Dáil, in the Seanad and on local authorities. This further form of injustice is an inequality in the distribution of power and influence. It blocks women's participation in society by excluding them from decision making positions and processes.

Again this is linked to the other two forms of injustice. Inequality of status and standing diminishes influence. It justifies and enables exclusion of women from decision making. Exclusion from decision making enables economic inequality as it means policy making, in the absence of women decision makers, ends up perpetuating rather than challenging issues such as the distribution of paid and unpaid work between women and men.

Inequality is shaped around these three interlinked forms of injustice—economic, cultural and political. However, the policy response to this inequality is fragmented into two different strands. This makes for an incoherent, divisive and ineffective response to inequality.

This fragmented approach allows governments to pick and choose which strand of policy for equality to prioritise. This is evident in looking back over the past decade of economic boom. There was no focus on redistribution. The unstated assumption was that a rising tide would lift all boats and no particular new policy intervention was required to redistribute resources. As a result, economic inequality persisted at a high level over this period of economic boom. In 2008, 28 per cent of all income earned was earned by a mere 6 per cent of the Irish population (Colm Keena, *The Irish Times*, 5 March 2009). It is estimated that the top 1 per cent of the population now holds 20 per cent of the wealth in Ireland, and that the top 5 per cent holds 40 per cent of the wealth (*A Better Ireland is Possible*, Community Platform, 2008).

However, this period of economic boom was also when the Government introduced equality legislation to prohibit discrimination in the workplace and vocational training and in the provision of goods and services across nine different grounds. The policy focus was on identity and recognition—the cultural field. Little was done in relation to economic or indeed political inequalities. Progress on equality was made but it was uneven. Under cover of the uneven progress made, policy failed to address key areas of economic and political inequality.

Any social movement for a more equal society is weakened by this fragmented approach to inequality. Civil society organisations tend to focus their work either on issues of poverty and an agenda of redistribution or on issues of identity and an agenda of recognition. There are organisations that have sought to address both forms of injustice. However, work on redistribution issues and work on recognition issues end up as distinct areas of activity, analysis and skills. A fragmented approach thus divides any potential social movement for a more equal society.

The interlinked nature of the three different forms of injustice that underpin inequality cannot be addressed by a fragmented approach. It is not possible to address any one form of injustice in isolation from the other forms of injustice that can be causal factors for the one issue being addressed. Initiatives to tackle poverty, for example, will be inadequate where they cannot simultaneously address issues of unequal status and influence which can be used to justify and contribute to poverty. This fragmented approach will not be able to identify or address the root causes of inequality. Any initiative taken will only be dealing with one part of a much wider picture. The inter-connected political, economic, cultural and social systems at play in the creation of inequality will not be exposed, challenged or changed.

A fragmented policy approach to inequality can only serve the interests of the powerful—those who have influence, those who hold the wealth and those who are afforded status and standing in society. It leads to uneven progress on equality. It fails to secure the change that is required in the way society is organised economically, culturally and politically so as to achieve equality. It divides civil society and any nascent social movement for a more equal society. It is now necessary and possible to imagine and design the institutions and policies that could achieve equality by addressing issues of redistribution of resources, of recognition of difference and of sharing of power and influence in an integrated and effective manner.

What should be done

A new statutory organisation underpinned by new equality legislation with a brief in relation to poverty, discrimination and the sharing of power and influence would be a valuable social dividend to secure from managing the present economic crisis. It would transform a low point into a turning point in the search for a more equal society. It would represent a political commitment to make a more coherent and effective impact on inequality and on the different forms of injustice that underpin inequality. A new focal point would thus be created for a societal drive to achieve equality and to eliminate poverty, discrimination and powerlessness. A source of new energy would be available to mobilise and support advocates by giving them new levers with which to promote equality in their organisations. A new profile to equality issues would result that would stimulate a new confidence and awareness of rights among those who experience disadvantage and discrimination. The challenge of equality to Irish society would be redefined in terms of enabling participation by all through eliminating injustices of poverty, discrimination and powerlessness.

The grounds covered in new equality legislation would need to be expanded to reflect this integrated approach to equality. In particular, a new ground of socio-economic status should be included. This would protect people from discrimination on the basis of their class. It is clear that there are significant levels of discrimination based on socio-economic status. The Central Statistics Office special survey on equality in 2005 found that 12.5 per cent of people aged eighteen and over said they had experienced discrimination in the preceding two years (Central Statistics Office, 2005a, *Quarterly National Household Survey, Equality Module*, Dublin). Almost one third of these people felt they had been discriminated against on grounds other than those covered by the equality legislation. The unemployed, trade union members and people educated to primary and lower secondary level were more likely to report discrimination on this 'other' ground. While this is not conclusive, it does point to socio-economic status as a ground on which discrimination is being widely experienced.

Discrimination would need to be redefined in the new equality legislation. The current equality legislation defines discrimination in terms of a person being treated less favourably than another person because of their identity, because they belong to one of the groups covered by the equality legislation. This definition would not be broad enough to capture the impact of injustice based on poverty or on powerlessness. A broader definition of discrimination in the equality legislation should include treatment of a person in a way that disadvantages them because of their membership of one of the grounds covered by the equality legislation. This would ensure that instances of stereotyping could be viewed as discrimination. It would mean that actions that economically disadvantage people because they are from groups covered by the equality legislation would be prohibited. Cases could also be taken where people from these groups were excluded from designated decision-making roles, such as on boards of statutory organisations, because of their membership of these groups.

The new legislation would need to be less reliant on individuals bringing forward cases of discrimination for its impact. It should be able to achieve change in the way organisations operate so as to prevent discrimination happening in the first place, and so as to secure a more active commitment to achieving equality within organisations. The new equality legislation should therefore place a duty on public sector organisations to have due regard to equality in carrying out their functions. It should require private sector organisations to be planned and systematic in their approach to equality, diversity and non-discrimination. These requirements would stimulate a process of organisational change across all sectors that would contribute to preventing discrimination and disadvantage, and to creating and sustaining a more equal society.

The new statutory equality body established by this legislation would need to integrate and go beyond the functions of both the Combat Poverty Agency and the Equality Authority. The functions of the new body should be to promote equality of outcome and to combat injustice in redistribution, recognition and the sharing of power and influence. It would have powers to support individuals to take cases under the legislation, to develop initiatives to support the achievement of equality of outcomes for groups experiencing inequality, to provide advice to Government on policy to promote equality of outcome, and to take action to build an understanding among the general public of equality and the need to combat inequality. The new equality body should be empowered to set and enforce standards for the new duties on public and private sector bodies to promote equality. Public sector bodies would need to be supported by the new equality body in assessing all policies for their impact on inequality. The new equality body should also have powers to investigate and make findings on patterns of injustice in redistribution, recognition and the sharing of power within organisations and within the wider society.

There would need to be particular emphasis on the independence of this new equality body. The board should no longer be appointed at the discretion of the relevant minister. A separate process to advertise for and recruit appropriate board members should be set in place by the Public Appointments Service. The new equality body should not be made accountable to a government department that it could be involved in litigation against. There is an interesting example in the legislation governing the Ombudsman for Children. This sets out that she shall be independent in carrying out her functions. It also requires her to attend before any committee of the Oireachtas to account for the general administration of her office. This could provide the basis for creating an accountability of bodies such as the new equality body to the Oireachtas rather than an individual government department.

New equality legislation and a new equality body would serve to drive and focus attention on creating a more equal society. However, it will not be able to operate in a vacuum. It will be most effective where it operates as part of a wider policy context committed to achieving equality and where it can interact with a wider social movement for equality.

A new development model

A wider policy context committed to achieving equality will be very different to the current model of economic and social development being pursued in Ireland. The neo-liberal economic policies that predominated during the boom times not only led to economic crisis but also failed to create a more equal society. They generated greater inequalities. If we want to live and work in a more equal society we must learn from this experience. We need to organise things differently. An alternative model of economic and social development is required based on an economy that is at the service of people and of society. It will involve a society that values equality and is organised on the basis of equality and respect between people and groups.

A time of economic recession and crisis is a time of change. It offers the opportunity to re-imagine the type of society we now want to create. There is the potential to shape a response to the crisis that could, in the longer term, lead to a society and an economy based on the principle of equality and committed to justice in redistribution, recognition and sharing of power and influence.

One personal gain from resigning from the Equality Authority was the freedom it has allowed me to engage in the search to define this alternative model of development. One way I have been able to do this has been as part of a new group called 'Is Féidir Linn'. This group is a form of grassroots think-tank made up of people who have been involved in community work, social inclusion, anti poverty, human rights and equality issues. The group initially formed out of a concern for issues facing community sector groups in their relations with the state. In particular, there were concerns about funding arrangements and about the state's attempts to control and minimise dissent from the sector. However as the economic recession has taken hold this focus has broadened into a shared concern to develop and promote a vision for an inclusive, equal and sustainable Ireland.

Equality is put forward by Is Féidir Linn as one of the core values that inform this vision. The group has published a manifesto for a model of development that 'contributes to equality for all groups and individuals in society in terms of the distribution of resources and services, the recognition of diversity and the exercise of influence' (*A Vision for an Inclusive, Equal, Sustainable Ireland*, Is Féidir Linn, June 2009). This manifesto sets out a wide range of goals and objectives to be pursued in what is an alternative model of economic and social development for Ireland.

Six guiding themes shape this alternative model put forward by Is Féidir Linn.

One guiding theme is the need to prioritise 'investment in high quality, efficient and effective public sector services'. Public sector services are under severe pressure. They are vilified in the media. They have been put forward by politicians almost as the source of the economic crisis and the parlous state of the public finances. These services are being damaged and diminished in the search for a solution to the economic crisis.

This is not good for equality. Public sector services have a critical contribution to make to achieving equality. The quality and accessibility of public sector services have a central impact on the well being of groups experiencing inequality. Investment in high quality, efficient and effective public sector services serves as an effective means of redistributing wealth and societal resources.

The public sector is challenged to reform. It should be more efficient. It should not be involved in so many discrimination cases under the Equal Status Acts. It should be more flexible in taking account of the diversity of groups it serves. It should be better at seeking to achieve equality for groups. Standards need to be set, monitored and enforced in all of these areas. Adequacy of provision must also be a key goal to be realised. This prioritisation of public sector services will require a higher level of taxation to ensure the revenue needed to secure this adequacy of service provision and to meet these standards in public sector service provision.

Another guiding theme is the importance of *universal access to key publicly funded services*. This becomes possible in the context of higher taxation for adequate public sector service provision. 'There should be publicly funded universal access to education, health and care services. There should be no public support for the private enhancement of these core rights'. Universal access to these services will remove any restriction on access to these services by means testing recipients or by insurance requirements on recipients.

Universal provision of a service enhances access and quality of the service as it is available to and used by all in society. It means that there are no arbitrary cut off points for publicly funded services that can limit access for people just above those income levels. Standards can slip where services only target groups experiencing inequality. People experiencing inequality often do not have the resources or the influence to sustain a demand for high quality and adequacy. In universal provision this demand is sustained by the powerful as well as those with less influence.

Universal provision of a service does need to take account of diversity. Public services should adapt and adjust their provision so that all groups in society can access and benefit from them. This ensures that public services address issues not only of redistribution but also of recognition. Universal provision of services has a further benefit in terms of recognition. It removes any stigma associated with dependence on publicly funded services. Means tested public services can serve the equality goal of redistribution. However, they can also act as a barrier to the equality goal of recognition where stigma leads to lower status and standing for those in receipt of public services. Universal provision of public services thus serves both redistribution and recognition.

Full employment is a third guiding theme in this alternative model of development. Full employment is central to the sustainability of the model. 'Policies and programmes should seek to achieve full employment where everyone can exercise their right to freely chosen, decently paid work and where employment standards are fully enforced'. Employment is a key source of security for people. It is central to enabling participation in society. It will underpin a more equal society. Policies and programmes also need to address the current unequal sharing of paid and unpaid work between men and women so that both men and women have the right to paid work and to care.

Income equality is another guiding theme which is related to employment and taxation policies. 'Tax and income policy should ensure minimum and maximum income standards. The highest income earners should have no more than ten times the income of the lowest earners'. Minimum income levels should be paid at a level that ensures people can have a standard of living that is adequate to support their full participation in society.

Media coverage of the recession has reflected significant public anger at the high levels of income and bonus payments paid to senior management in the financial sector. My own experience in the Equality Authority is that over the past decade income at the higher levels of the public service has also increased at an extraordinary rate. Benchmarking public sector pay has replicated private sector inequalities in the public sector. High pay and benefits for politicians has also been widely criticised. However, part of the response to the recession has been to attack minimum income levels and reduce social welfare rates. Attention is now required to defend minimum income and social welfare rates and to establish greater income equality through taxation and income caps on maximum income levels.

A fifth guiding theme is focused on *recognition* and the need for 'society and its institutions to appropriately and adequately value diversity in society and eliminate all forms of discrimination'. The new approach to diversity required starts with new equality legislation, alongside independent and adequately resourced statutory agencies to implement it.

Policies and programmes should be further developed with the capacity 'to eliminate violence and abuse targeted at specific groups in society'. Domestic violence is one obvious example to be addressed. Racist attacks, homophobic bullying in schools and abuse of older people in care have also been highlighted in recent times. Policies, programmes and standards are also required 'to eliminate stereotyping, in particular in all forms of media and advertising'.

This theme of recognition seeks to establish a new perspective on difference in Irish society. It is based on the need to value difference. Current responses to difference often define difference as a problem and require those deemed to be different to change their behavior or values. We can often render difference invisible and engage in a pretence that we are all the same. At best we promote a tolerance of difference which falls far short of mutual respect.

This need to value difference is not about creating an uncritical acceptance of all differences. It is about creating the conditions of equality within which groups can pursue equality of status and make their claim for recognition. This requires change. Organisational policies and practices cannot continue to be shaped by a single dominant norm. Democratic spaces need to be created to realise a dialogue of equals about difference and claims for recognition. In this way difference will be appropriately and adequately valued in practical terms.

Democracy is the final guiding theme with a particular emphasis on creating a democratic system that is both participatory and representative. There is a need to 'develop models of participatory democracy and specific supports to enable those experiencing poverty and inequality to participate in and influence decision making'. Particular attention is required to ensure that funding from private or public sources respects the independence of community organisations and enables these organisations to play advocacy roles. Community organisations have a valuable contribution to make to systems of participatory democracy.

Community organisations provide a space for people from groups that experience inequality to meet and to explore and identify their shared needs and interests. Community organisations offer a platform for these people to advocate for or to negotiate on these shared interests. They offer a voice to groups experiencing inequality. This is a key foundation for participatory democracy. It is of concern that statutory sector funders have sought to marginalise this advocacy. Funding conditions prevent organisations from engaging in advocacy. The funding available increasingly channels community organisations into service provision activities. Budgets have been threatened where groups engage in advocacy. A restructuring of funding from community development has recently reduced funding to community organisations and compromised their independence. This marginalisation of advocacy by statutory funders undermines democracy. It also serves as a barrier to the emergence of a strong social movement for equality.

A new social movement

An alternative model of economic and social development with a capacity to create a more equal society will not emerge without the support and advocacy of a broad social movement. This is required to challenge and change the current balance of forces in society which remains in favour of maintaining and repairing the current model of development—a model that has not served equality and a model that has been the source of economic crisis.

This social movement for an alternative model of development will need to involve new alliances across civil society. These alliances should involve community organisations, trade unions, environmental organisations, cultural bodies, developing world agencies, student organisations, political parties and more. Many organisations in these different parts of civil society already seek change for greater equality in the way Irish society is organised. All such organisations could come together under the banner of a more equal, sustainable and inclusive Ireland. However, these types of alliances will not be easily created. These different parts of civil society are fragmented into their own specific policy areas. Each has its own traditions, language and way of operating. It will take creativity, flexibility and patience to manage this diversity. It is, though, a diversity that could lend itself to a powerful and innovative alliance for change.

This social movement will need to embed these values of equality, sustainability and inclusion in Irish culture. These are values that need to form part of a societal common sense if we are to build an alternative model of development. They need to be the values we reach for when we seek to make a judgment about where our society is at, and what now needs to be done to improve our society or to find a way out of the economic crisis. These are the values that should give a new balance to the predominant value currently accorded to economic competitiveness in public debate on the economic crisis. Currently policy and strategy prioritise economic competitiveness over inclusion, sustainability or equality. This is not good for society. It is not even good for economic development.

The case for equality

The moral case for equality is strong. Equality affirms human dignity and worth. Discrimination diminishes human dignity. Disadvantage denies human worth. However, equality is not only good for people who experience inequality. Equality is good for business and economic development. Equality is good for almost everyone in society.

The business case for equality underpins the need for equality to be a focus in any policy response to the economic crisis. International evidence demonstrates that equality is good for business. Workplace policies in relation to positive action and equality enhance organisational performance. Diversity in the membership of top management teams helps companies do better. Diverse work groups can be a source of creativity and innovation in organisations (*The Business Impact of Equality and Diversity, The international evidence*, Kathy Monks, Equality Authority and National

Centre for Partnership and Performance, 2007).

Irish research reinforces these findings. Economic and Social Research Institute researchers used a national survey of over five thousand employees to explore the business case for equality. They found that having a workplace equality policy is strongly associated with lower levels of work stress for employees. Workplace equality policies were also found to be strongly associated with higher levels of job satisfaction and organisational commitment of employees. They concluded that given these effects, equality policies are likely to have a positive impact on organisational performance and hence to be of benefit to employers (*Equality at Work? Workplace equality policies, flexible working arrangements and the quality of work*, P. O'Connell and H. Russell, Equality Authority, 2005).

The business case for equality has also been quantified in an Irish context (*New Models of High Performance Work Systems, The business case for strategic human resource management, partnership and diversity and equality systems*, P. Flood et al, Equality Authority and National Centre for Partnership and Performance, 2008). This research was based on 132 medium to large companies in Ireland which were drawn from '*The Irish Times* Top 1000 Companies'. It explored the variation in labour productivity, workforce innovation and employee retention between these companies. It found that having equality and diversity systems in companies accounted for 6.5 per cent of the variance in labour productivity, for 7.9 per cent of the variance in workforce innovation, and for 4.4 per cent of the variance in employee turnover. Equality and diversity systems had a quantifiable economic benefit for these companies through greater labour productivity, higher workforce innovation and decreased employee turnover.

A strong economic case for equality has also been researched and advanced. In late 2009 the Swedish Ministry of Integration and Gender Equality financed research on the economic case for gender equality as part of their Presidency of the European Union (*Gender Equality, Economic Growth and Employment*, Asa Lofstrom, Department of Economics, Umea University). This research found that there are major economic gains to be made from gender equality and in particular from a gender equal labour market. It concluded that 'Calculations of a maximum value of these gains shows that there is a potential for increased Gross Domestic Product of between 15% and 45% in the European Union member states'.

Richard Wilkinson and Kate Pickett have published research on the societal case for equality (*The Spirit Level, Why more equal societies almost always do better*, R. Wilkinson and K. Pickett, Allen Lane, 2009). They put forward compelling evidence that income inequalities are at the root of a wide range of health and social problems in society. They compare the performance of 23 different countries on the basis of income inequality data. The USA, Portugal, Britain and Singapore emerge as the most unequal in terms of income distribution. Japan and Sweden emerge as the most equal. They also compare the performance of fifty different USA states on the basis of income inequality data. Their findings in these two different settings are remarkably similar.

Levels of trust between people, life expectancy, educational attainment and social mobility are all found to be lower in the countries and states with greater income inequality. Mental illness rates, use of illegal drugs, obesity levels, teenage pregnancy rates, levels of violence and rates of imprisonment are all found to be higher in the countries and states with greater income inequality. They note that these health and social problems are not caused by 'the society not being rich enough (or even by being too rich) but by the scale of material differences between people within each society being too big'.

They conclude that the vast majority of the population in these countries and states is harmed by greater inequality. The harm is not confined to those people who have the lowest income levels. The scale and prevalence of the health and social problems identified demonstrate that they are experienced by a far wider group than those living in poverty. The overall impact of these health and social problems is felt by an even wider group than those who directly experience the specific problems. Societal well being is diminished by inequality.

All of this research clarifies that we need to stop viewing equality as a cost and begin to understand it as an investment. Economic recession should trigger an increased focus on equality rather than being used as a cover to dismantle our capacity to promote and advance equality. Investment in a new statutory equality body and the enactment of more ambitious equality legislation is necessary if we are to underpin business performance, economic development and societal well being. New economic and social policies based on equality are required if we are to emerge from this economic recession. We cannot afford to disarm the thrust for a more equal society. We cannot afford the coup at the Equality Authority and the analysis that it reflected.

Index

Sun 68

Sunday Independent 68, 69, 70, 71, 72, 81

Sunday Times 98, 107

Sunday Tribune, 75, 81, 82

Supreme Court 67, 90–2

Travellers
  case under Equal Status Acts 4-5
  ground of discrimination 3, 31, 76
  licensed premises 74, 75
  and racism viii
  segregation 30

Ulster Bank 21, 35

victimisation case 28, 35

Village Magazine 116

Vintners Federation of Ireland 74–82

Walsh, Dick 72

Walsh, Kathy 117

Waters, John 108, 111

Waters, Noel 88

Westmeath EQUAL 39

Westport Vintners Association 74, 78

White, Dan 77

White, Trevor 73

Wilkinson, Richard 135

women, and forms of injustice 119–20